MASTERS OF ART

THE STORY
OF SCULPTURE

FRANCESCA ROMEI

◆

ILLUSTRATED BY
GIACINTO GAUDENZI

PETER BEDRICK BOOKS
NEW YORK

DoGi

Produced by
Donati Giudici Associati, Florence
Original title:
La Scultura dall'antichità ad oggi
Text:
Francesca Romei
Illustrations:
Giacinto Gaudenzi
Picture research and
coordination of foreign editions:
Caroline Godard
Art direction:
Oliviero Ciriaci
Page design:
Luca Theodoli
Laura Davis
Editing:
Enza Fontana
English translation:
Deborah Misuri-Charkham
Editor, English-language edition:
Ruth Nason
Typesetting:
Ken Alston – A.J. Latham Ltd

© 1995 Donati Giudici Associati s.r.l.,
Florence, Italy
English language text © 1995 by
Macdonald Young Books/
Peter Bedrick Books
First published in the United States
in 1995 by
PETER BEDRICK BOOKS
2112 Broadway
New York, N.Y. 10023

Library of Congress - Cataloging-in-
Publication Data

Romei, Francesca
    The story of sculpture: from
prehistory to the present / text by
Francesca Romei; illustrated by
Gaudenzi, Giacinto. – 1st ed.
    p. cm. –(Masters of Art)
    Simultaneously published in
Italian under title: La scultura
dell'antichità ad oggi
    Includes index.
    ISBN 0-87226-316-9
    1. Sculpture–History. I. Title.
    II. Series: Masters of art
(Peter Bedrick Books)
    NB60. R57 1995
    730'.9–dc20   95-7006 CIP

Printed in Italy by
Giunti Industrie Grafiche, Prato
Photolitho:
Venanzoni D.T.P., Florence
Second printing,1997

◆ ABOUT THIS BOOK

Some of the double-page spreads in this book deal with a particular period from the history of art. For instance, there are sections on the Stone Age, classical Greece and Rome, Romanesque and Gothic sculpture, the Baroque, and the 19th and 20th centuries. Other double-page sections look at great world civilizations and the sculpture they produced. China, India, Japan, the Americas, Oceania and Africa are all included. To represent each historical period and culture, each double page focuses on a key event, style, set of works or single artist. Detailed background information complements the central topic on each spread. Finally, some double-page sections in the book, such as those on Working in wood and Sculpture in terracotta, are devoted to different working methods used by sculptors. These sections also take a certain event or artist as their focus.

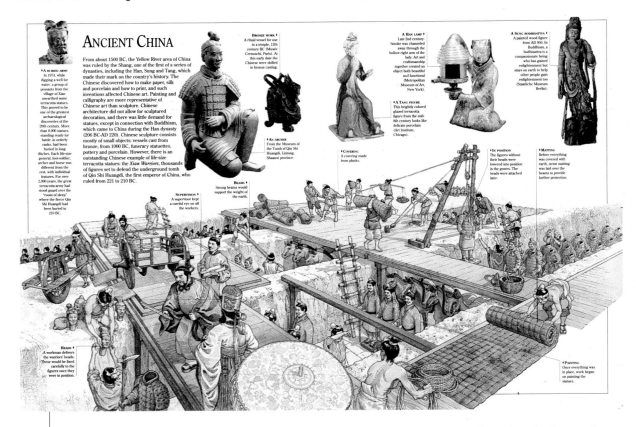

The large central illustration represents the main theme.

The smaller pictures, captions and text provide a wealth of

complementary background information.

CREDITS

The original and previously unpublished illustrations in this book may not be reproduced without the prior permission of Donati Giudici Associati, who hold the copyright. The illustration on pages 32-33 is by Sergio, and that on page 57 is by Gianni Mazzoleni. All other illustrations are by Giacinto Gaudenzi.

Note: In the credits below, the photographs on each page are listed alphabetically, reading from left to right and from top to bottom.

P. 5: *a, b* Carlo Cantini, Florence. P. 6: *a* Naturhistorisches Museum, Vienna; *b* Alinari/Giraudon. P. 7: *a, b* Collection photothèque du Musée de l'Homme, Paris (photo D. Destable); *c* Alinari/Giraudon; *d, e* Réunion des Musées Nationaux, Paris. P. 8: *a, c* Museo Egizio, Turin; *b* Egyptian Museum, Berlin. P. 9: *a, b* Alinari/Giraudon; *c* British Museum, London. P. 10: *a* Alinari/Giraudon; *b* Electa, Milan. P. 11: *a* Scala, Florence. P. 12: *a* British Museum, London. P. 13: *a* DoGi, Florence. P. 14: *a* Alinari/Giraudon. P. 15: *a, b* Alinari/Giraudon; *c* DoGi, Florence. P. 16: *a* Alinari/Giraudon; *b* Panini, Modena; *c* Réunion des Musées Nationaux, Paris; *d* Scala, Florence. P. 17: *a, e* Studio Kopperman, Gauting press, Munich; *b* Réunion des Musées Nationaux, Paris; *c* Scala, Florence; *d* Arris/Araldo di Lucca, Rome. P. 18: *a, b, c* Scala, Florence. P. 19: *a, b* Arris/Araldo di Lucca, Rome. P. 20: *a* Panini, Modena; *b, c, j* Arris/Araldo di Lucca, Rome; *d, e* Scala, Florence; *f, g, h, i* Münzkabinett, Berlin. P. 21: *a* Réunion des Musées Nationaux, Paris; *b* Alinari/Giraudon; *c* Scala, Florence; *d, g* Arris/Araldo di Lucca, Rome; *e, i* Panini, Modena; *f* Marco Ricci, Rome; *h* Museo nazionale romano, Rome. P. 22: *a, b* Roberto Micheli, Milan; *c* Museo Cernuschi, Paris. P. 23: *a* Art Institute, Chicago; *b* Metropolitan Museum of Art, New York; *c* Staatliche Museen, Berlin. P. 24: *a* Patna Museum, Patna; *b* Bridgeman Art Library, London; *c* Archaeological Museum, Sarnath. P. 25: *a, c* Archaeological Museum, Sarnath; *d* National Museum, New Delhi; *e, f* DoGi, Florence. P. 26: *a, b* Peter Willi, Paris. P. 27: *a* Peter Willi, Paris; *b* Alinari/Giraudon; *c* Biblioteca Laurentiana, Florence. P. 28: *a, b* Peter Willi, Paris; *c* Alinari/Giraudon. P. 29: *a, b* Alinari/Giraudon. P. 30: *a* Réunion des Musées Nationaux, Paris; *b* Alinari/Giraudon; *c, d, e* Scala, Florence. P. 31: *a, b* Alinari/Giraudon; *c* Scala, Florence; *d* DoGi (Mario Quattrone); *e* the author; *f* Eric Lessing, Vienna. P. 32: *a* Kofukuji, Nara; *b* Todai-ji, Nara. P. 33: *a, b* Horui-ji, Nara; *c* De Agostini, Novara; *d* Mora-ji, Nara; *e* Todai-ji, Nara; *f* Thames and Hudson, London. P. 35: *a* Eric Lessing, Vienna; *b* Foto Fontani, Florence; *c* Alinari/Giraudon; *d* Scala, Florence. P. 36: *a* DoGi (Mario Quattrone). P. 37: *a* Scala, Florence; *b* Vorderasiatisches Museum, Berlin; *c* Museo archeologico, Tarquinia; *d* Alinari/Giraudon. P. 38: *a, b* the author; *c* Museo Pigorini, Rome. P. 39: *a, b, c, d, f* Museo Pigorini, Rome; *e* the author. P. 40: *a* Museo archeologico, Tarquinia; *b* DoGi (Mario Quattrone); *c* Marco Ricci, Rome; *d* Musei Vaticani, Rome. P. 41: *a* British Museum, London; *b, c, e, f, h* DoGi (Mario Quattrone); *d, g, i* Marco Ricci, Rome; *j* Scala, Florence. P. 43: *a, b, c* Carlo Cantini, Florence; *d* British Museum, London. P. 44: *a* DoGi (Mario Quattrone);

b Victoria and Albert Museum, London; *c, d, e, f* Carlo Cantini, Florence.
P. 45: *a, b, c* Carlo Cantini, Florence; *d, f, g* Carlo Cantini, Florence; *e* DoGi (Mario Quattrone). P. 46: *a* Alinari/Giraudon; *b* Victoria and Albert Museum, London; *c* DoGi (Mario Quattrone). P. 47: *a, c* Alinari/Giraudon; *b* Eric Lessing, Vienna; *d, e, f, g* DoGi (Mario Quattrone). P. 48: *a* Alinari/Giraudon. P. 49: *a, d* Scala, Florence; *b* DoGi; *c* Peter Willi, Paris. P. 50: *a, b, c, d, e* Cabinet des dessins, Paris. P. 52: *a* Plaster Casts Gallery, Possagno; *b* Arris/Araldo di Lucca, Rome. P. 53: *a* Alinari/Giraudon; *b* Plaster Casts Gallery, Possagno. P. 54: *a, b* Peter Willi, Paris; *c* Musée national des techniques, Paris; *d* Panini, Modena; *e, f* Public Library, New York; *g* Alinari/Giraudon. P. 55: *a, c* Réunion des Musées Nationaux, Paris; *b, d* Peter Willi, Paris; *e* Panini, Modena; *f, g* Alinari/Giraudon. P. 56: *a* British Museum, London; *b* Museo Pigorini, Rome; *c* Scala, Florence. P. 57: *a* Staatliche Museen, Berlin; *b* Bridgeman Art Library, London; *c* Antonio Quattrone, Florence; *d* Museum of Primitive Art, New York. P. 58: *a, b, c, d, j* Metropolitan Museum of Art, New York; *e, f, g, i* Alinari/Giraudon; *h* Museo Pigorini, Rome.
P. 59: *a, b, e* Bridgeman Art Library, London; *c, f* Alinari/Giraudon; *d, k* National Museum, Lagos; *g, h* Metropolitan Museum of Art, New York; *i* Barbier-Müller Museum, Geneva; *j* Galerie Beyeler, Basel. P. 60: *a, j* Sonnabend Collection, New York; *b* Musée Matisse, Nice; *c* Kunsthaus, Zurich; *d, e* Centre G. Pompidou, Paris; Bridgeman Art Library, London; *g, h* Réunion des Musées Nationaux, Paris; *i* Maeght Foundation, Saint-Paul-de-Vence (photo Claude Germain); *k* Sidney Janis Gallery, New York; *l* Jeanne-Claude Christo Collection, New York (photo Harry Shurk). P. 61: *a, d, h* Alinari/Giraudon; *b* Bridgeman Art Library, London; *c* D.R. (rights reserved); *e, f* Foto Descharnes & Descharnes; *g* Centre G. Pompidou, Paris; *i* Museum of Modern Art, New York; *j* Galleria Fonte d'Abisso, Milan; *k, l* Musée d'art moderne et d'art contemporain, Nice (photo Muriel Anssens); *m* Skira.
P. 62: *a* Carlo Nicoli, Carrara. P. 63: *a* Balthazar Korab, Troy.

The pictures of works by Henry Moore (pp. 35, 60), Max Ernst (p. 59), Alexander Calder (p. 63), César (pp. 61, 62), Claes Oldenburg, Henri Matisse, Pablo Picasso, Marcel Duchamp, Andy Warhol, George Segal, Christo (p. 60), Constantin Brancusi, Amedeo Modigliani, Umberto Boccioni, Raoul Haussman, Hans Arp, Meret Oppenheim, Salvador Dali, Robert Smithson (p. 61) have been reproduced with the authorization of the Società italiana degli autori ed editori, 1995. © Succession Matisse by SIAE 1995.

Cover photographs: *a, b, g, k* Alinari/Giraudon; *c* Museo Pigorini, Rome; *d, f* Bridgeman Art Library, London; *e, l* DoGi (Mario Quattrone); *h* Collection photothèque du Musée de L'Homme, Paris (photo D. Destable); *i* Museo Egizio, Turin; *j* Roberto Micheli, Milan.
Cover illustrations and frontispiece: Giacinto Gaudenzi.

All efforts have been made to trace the copyright holders of all the illustrations included in this book. If any omissions have been made, DoGi will be pleased to correct this at reprint.

CONTENTS

SCULPTURE

There are two basic ways of making a sculpture. The sculptor can use a soft material, such as clay, wax or plaster, and shape it into a figure or object. The sculptor's hands are the main tool for this work, and material can be both removed and added to make the shape required. Alternatively, the sculptor may begin with a block of hard material, such as wood, stone or ivory. In this case, tools like hammers and chisels are needed, and the figure is made by removing material from the block, by chipping and carving. To make a sculpture from metal, such as copper or bronze, the sculptor pours molten metal into a mold, which has been produced using an image made by one of the two basic methods. This is called casting. Shown here are some of the tools traditionally used by sculptors for first rough-shaping an image and then working on the detail.

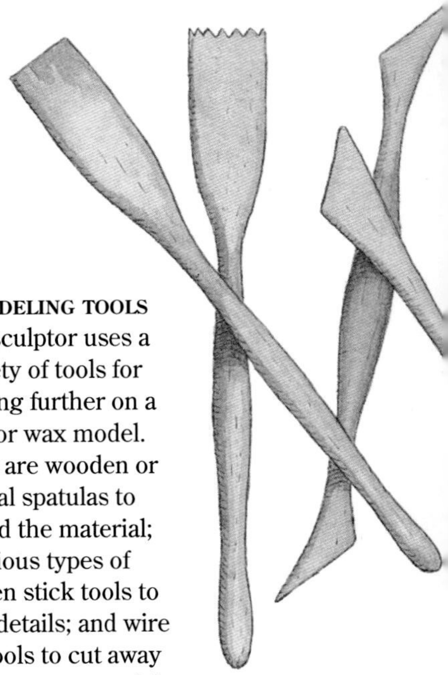

Spatulas.

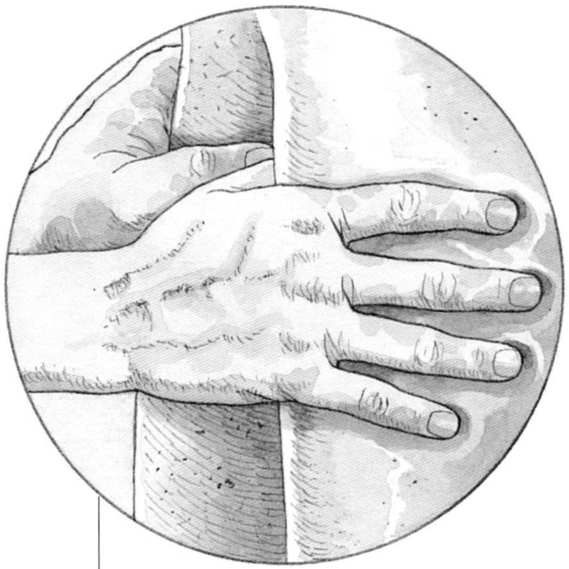

♦ MODELING TOOLS
The sculptor uses a variety of tools for working further on a clay or wax model. There are wooden or metal spatulas to spread the material; various types of wooden stick tools to model details; and wire loop tools to cut away or hollow out material.

♦ HANDS
Sculptors modeling in a material like clay or wax use their hands to rough-shape a figure or object.

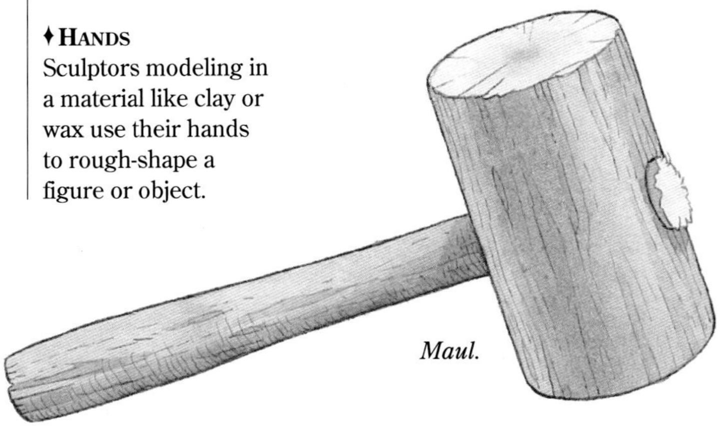

Maul.

♦ SOFT STONE
A light and delicate touch is needed for sculpting soft and crumbly stone like sandstone. The sculptor therefore uses wooden mauls and wooden-handled chisels to deaden the blows so that the stone does not break into pieces.

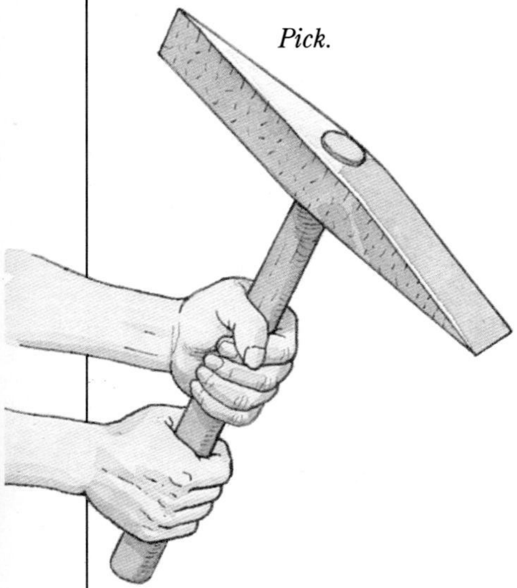

Pick.

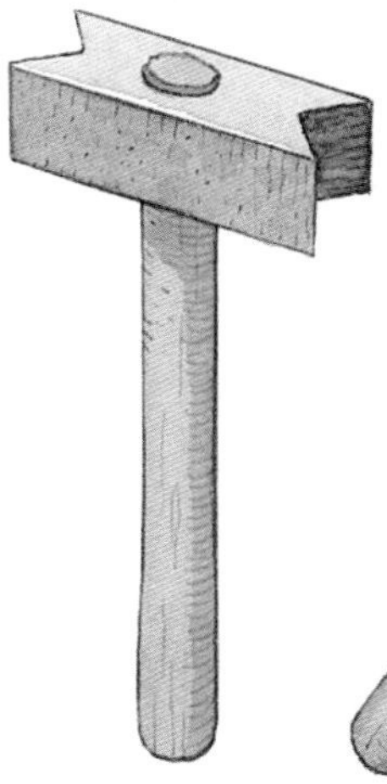

Concave-headed mallet.

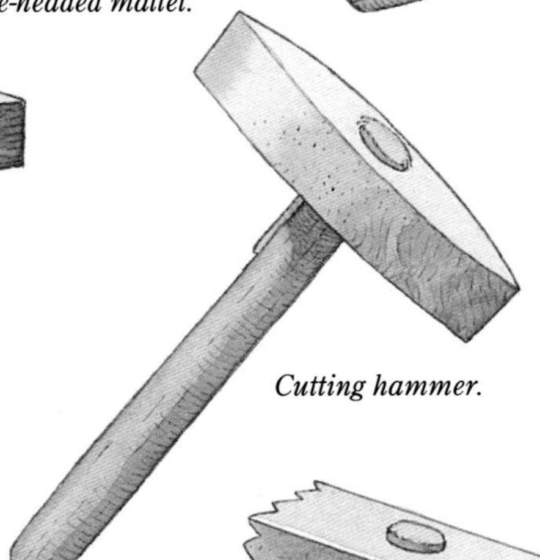

Cutting hammer.

Chisel.

♦ CHISELS
Having rough-shaped the statue, the sculptor uses hammers and mauls and chisels for chipping or carving. These vary according to whether the material is hard, semi-hard or soft, and according to the detail and finish the sculptor wants.

♦ AXES AND HAMMERS
The sculptor begins with a block of hard stone or wood, which must be turned into the rough shape of the intended statue or figure. This preliminary rough-shaping is done with tools such as axes and hammers. The sculptor holds these with both hands, and strikes and cuts the stone.

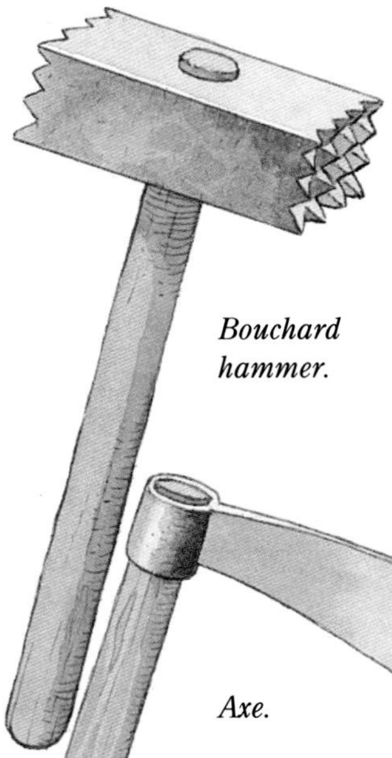

Bouchard hammer.

Chisel.

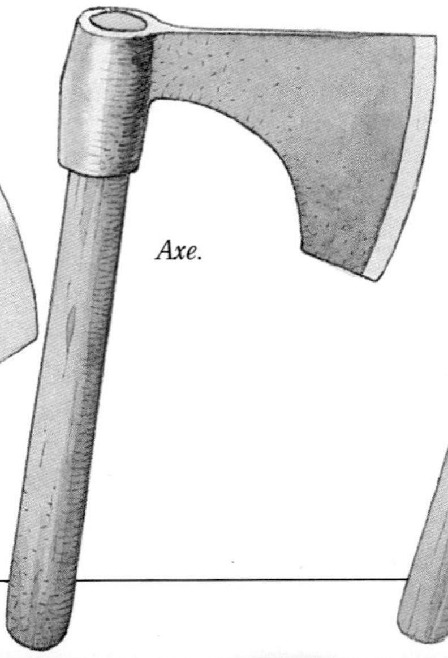

Axe.

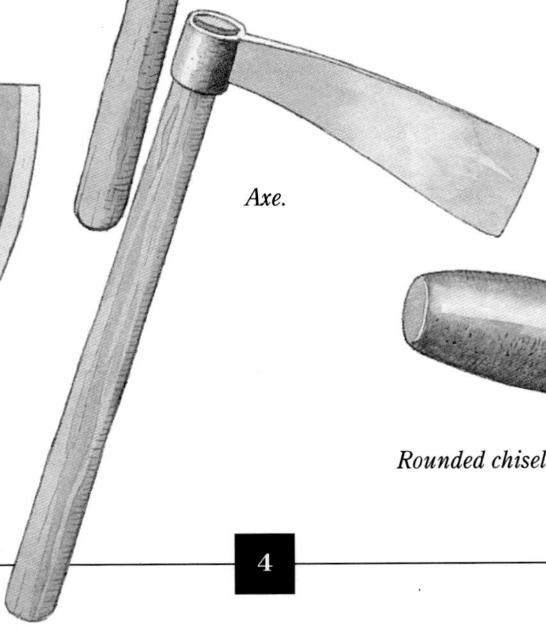

Axe.

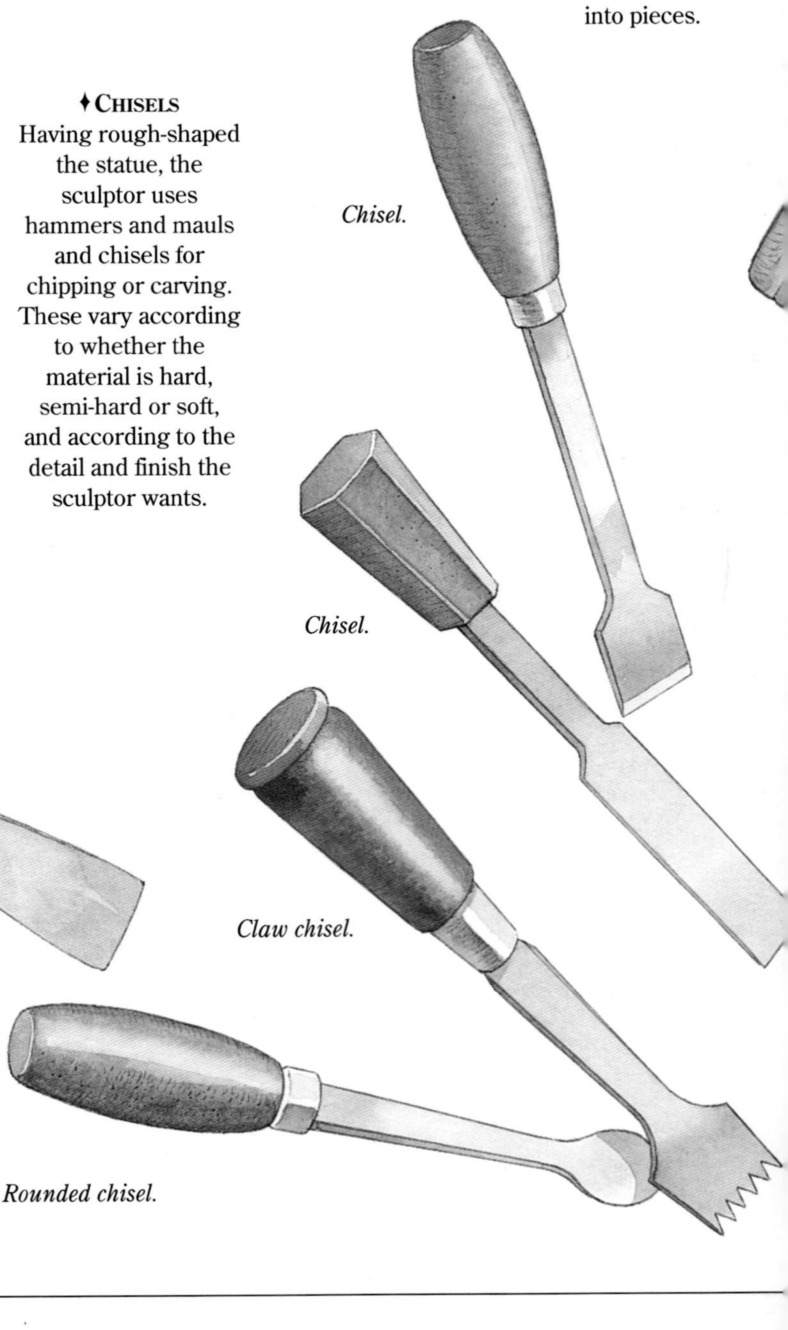

Claw chisel.

Adze.

Rounded chisel.

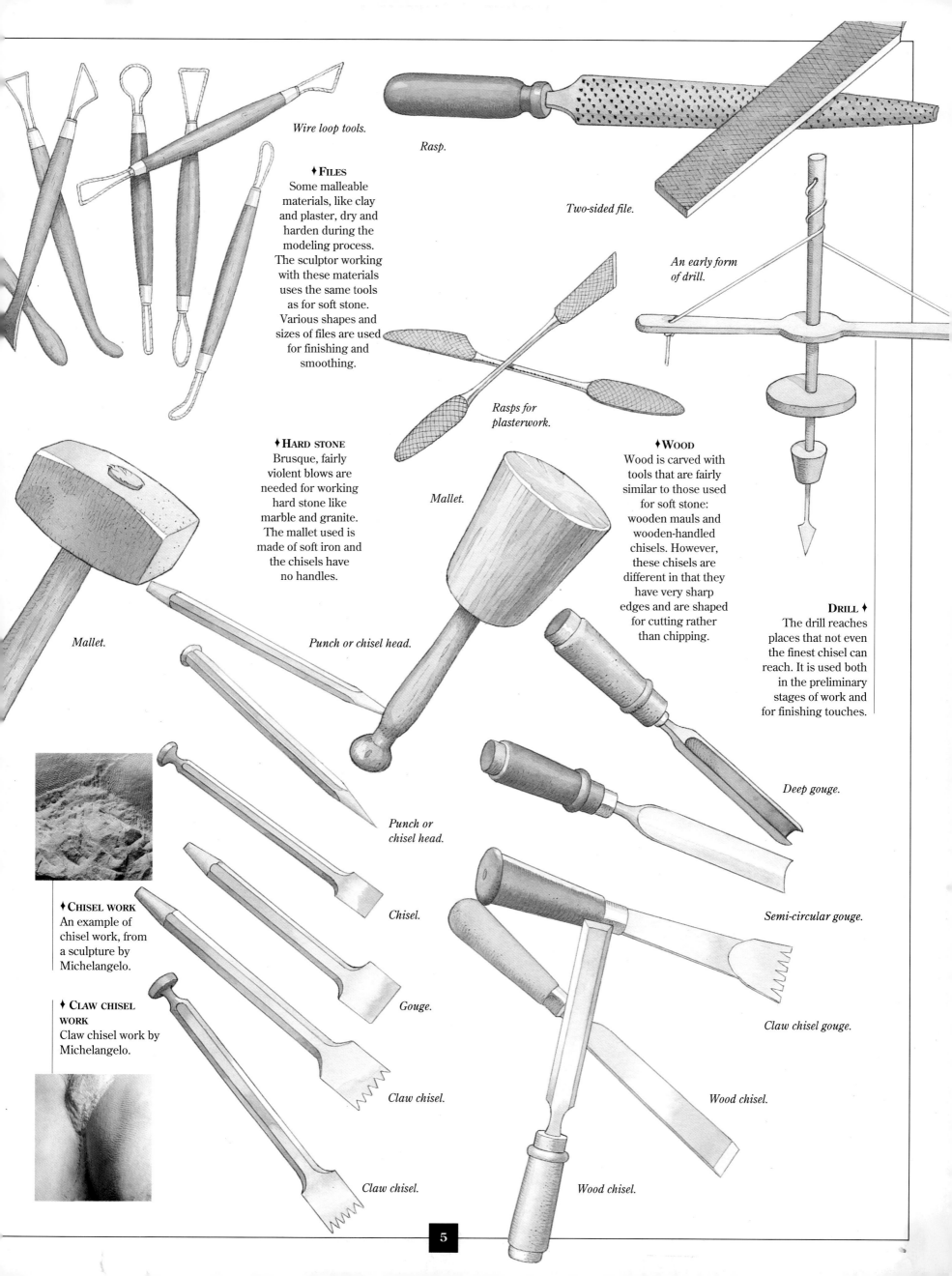

Wire loop tools.

Rasp.

Two-sided file.

♦ **FILES**
Some malleable materials, like clay and plaster, dry and harden during the modeling process. The sculptor working with these materials uses the same tools as for soft stone. Various shapes and sizes of files are used for finishing and smoothing.

An early form of drill.

Rasps for plasterwork.

♦ **HARD STONE**
Brusque, fairly violent blows are needed for working hard stone like marble and granite. The mallet used is made of soft iron and the chisels have no handles.

Mallet.

♦ **WOOD**
Wood is carved with tools that are fairly similar to those used for soft stone: wooden mauls and wooden-handled chisels. However, these chisels are different in that they have very sharp edges and are shaped for cutting rather than chipping.

DRILL ♦
The drill reaches places that not even the finest chisel can reach. It is used both in the preliminary stages of work and for finishing touches.

Mallet.

Punch or chisel head.

Punch or chisel head.

Deep gouge.

♦ **CHISEL WORK**
An example of chisel work, from a sculpture by Michelangelo.

Chisel.

Semi-circular gouge.

Gouge.

Claw chisel gouge.

♦ **CLAW CHISEL WORK**
Claw chisel work by Michelangelo.

Claw chisel.

Wood chisel.

Claw chisel.

Wood chisel.

THE STONE AGE

The first humans drew outlines of animals on rock, roughly sculpted stone, and molded figures from clay. These early works of art often had a magic or religious function. Drawing and painting animals inside a cave was a magical way of luring them there, so that they could be captured. Making female figures with exaggeratedly large breasts and hips was meant to bring good fortune on fertility, pregnancy and motherhood. Many religions and mythologies use the image of sculpting to explain how the first humans were created. In the Bible story of the creation, God created Adam from clay and gave him the breath of life. The Babylonian god Enki created men and women in the same way, so that they could work the land instead of the gods. In Egyptian myth, man was modeled on a potter's wheel and, in Greek myth, humans were clay images fashioned by Prometheus. The scientific story of human evolution is exciting in a different way. Archaeologists have made amazing discoveries of sculptures done by humans 20,000 years ago.

✦ MAKING TOOLS

What distinguished the first human beings from other animals was their ability to make tools. First of all they used stone. By thirty thousand years ago, in the Palaeolithic or Old Stone Age, people were skilled at striking one stone against another to make sharp-edged flakes. These almond-shaped flintstones were used to make spears and arrows and to engrave the first outlines into rock. Thousands of years passed before humans developed their manual ability further and began to model clay.

✦ FIGURES

Many images of women shaped like this one have been found at Stone Age sites throughout Europe. The best-known (left) is the *Willendorf Venus* (Naturhistorisches Museum, Vienna), which was found in Austria. It dates from 20,000 BC and archaeologists presume that it was a fertility goddess. It is 11.5 cm (4.3 in) high and was painted with red ochre.

✦ CLAY BISON

A model of the clay bison found in the Pyrenees (Musée des Antiquités Nationales, Saint-Germain-en-Laye).

- *Homo Sapiens* (35,000-100,000 years ago)
- *Homo Erectus* (500,000-1.6 million years ago)
- *Homo Habilis* (1-2 million years ago)
- *Australopithecus* (1-4 million years ago)

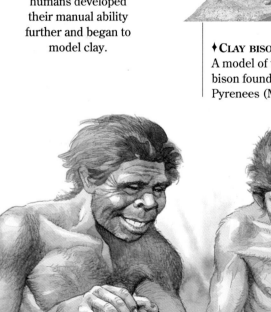

✦ THE EARLIEST SCULPTORS

The drawing on the left shows what the very first sculptors might have looked like. In 1912, the Bégouën brothers discovered the work of such people in the Pyrenees. Two bison, each about 50 cm (20 in) long, had been modeled in clay. The sculptors had taken great care in showing details of the faces and fur.

♦ STONE AGE FINDS
Archaeologists refer to the Old Stone Age (the Palaeolithic) and the New Stone Age (the Neolithic), when people began to settle. Many objects from the Palaeolithic Age have been found in the Pyrenees. The Neolithic culture began along the rivers Nile, Tigris and Euphrates. Tools from this age are made of polished stone.

♦ A MODERN-LOOKING SCULPTURE
This small sculpture from 20,000 BC, known as *Lespugue's Venus* (Musée de l'Homme, Paris), is made from ivory. It is a different shape from other female images of this time, and looks more like a modern sculpture.

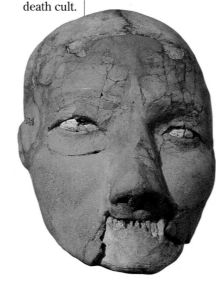

JERICHO ♦
Jericho in modern-day Jordan is the site of the oldest known human settlement. Finds of skulls covered in clay, from c.7000 BC, are evidence of a death cult.

HUNTING ♦
Stone Age artists depicted the animals they wanted to capture. The species portrayed, such as bison, deer, horse and ibex, are all edible. The bison here (Musée des Antiquités Nationales, Saint-Germain-en-Laye) was engraved on a reindeer horn. It decorates the head of a spear thrower and was meant to magically guide the spear towards its target.

♦ HISTORY
It was during the last Ice Age on earth, from about 1 million to 10,000 years ago, that people created the first sculptures. To begin with, they scratched pictures in stone or on fragments of bone or animal horn. Then they carved rock so that the picture was raised from the surface. Today this kind of sculpture is called low-relief, or bas-relief. Lastly, the Old Stone Age people carved small, completely rounded figures.

Our knowledge of Old Stone Age sculpture is based on archaeological finds of flint knives and blocks of stone left in sheltered places, apparently waiting to be worked.
As the ice thawed, from about 15,000 years ago, people abandoned their cave dwellings and their migratory way of life. They began to live by farming and rearing animals, and lived in more settled communities.

YOUNG GIRL ♦
Despite the absence of eyes and mouth, this small ivory head (Musée des Antiquités Nationales, Saint-Germain-en-Laye) from 20,000 BC is extraordinarily expressive.

It was in the New Stone Age that people first made terracotta statues, pots and domestic utensils. Terracotta is clay modeled and then fired in a kiln. This makes it hard and permanent.

♦ THE FIRST HUMANS
Humans are thought to have evolved from *Australopithecus*, a creature that lived in Africa and walked on two legs. *Homo Habilis* apparently used some very rough stone tools. *Homo Erectus* became expert at making stone tools and spread from Africa to southern Europe. *Homo Sapiens* developed the ability to create sculptures.

BEFORE IRON

Many sculptures from thousands of years ago, for example, from ancient Egypt, Babylonia and Assyria, are not completely free-standing. The sculptor has shown some parts, perhaps the head, from all sides, but much of the figure sticks out only slightly from the stone from which it is carved. Sculptors at this time also treated each view of a figure independently: they sculpted the front and the side views separately, rounding off the corner between them. This style is not a sign that the artists did not understand three-dimensional figures. It is rather a result of the tools and techniques that were available. Artists in ancient times used tools made of bronze or other alloys. These were relatively soft metals, which bent easily, and therefore tools made from them were not suited for digging deeply into stone. The limitations of the tools forced sculptors to produce great cube-shaped figures in a kind of low-relief. Not until the Iron Age could they make completely rounded sculptures.

CUBE STATUE ♦
Only the head of this figure from 1465 BC (Egyptian Museum, Berlin) stands out from the black granite block. The sculptor has shown the front face only.

LOW-RELIEF ♦
The ancient Egyptian sculptor engraved these figures carrying offerings (Museo Egizio, Turin) in limestone. The figures are slightly raised from the surface (in low-relief).

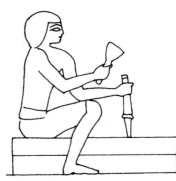

♦ AN EGYPTIAN SCULPTOR
A painted-wood figure of a sculptor from ancient Egypt (Museo Egizio, Turin). There were no work benches in ancient Egypt, and so the sculptor held the piece as he worked on it. He rough-shaped the stone with a hatchet, then used a mallet and chisel, and a scraper to finish the work. He struck the surface of the stone with a series of right-angled blows, using progressively smaller chisel heads. The tools available at this time were not strong enough for digging deeply with neat, slanting blows.

♦ THE METHOD USED
Ancient Egyptian statues that were left unfinished give an idea of the method used by the sculptors. These drawings are reconstructions of some of the stages of work. Having squared the block of stone, the sculptor drew the figure in ink on all four sides. Then, following the outlines, he rough-shaped the stone and removed layer after layer, finishing off as he went. The four sides of the statue therefore progressed simultaneously.

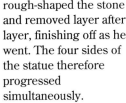
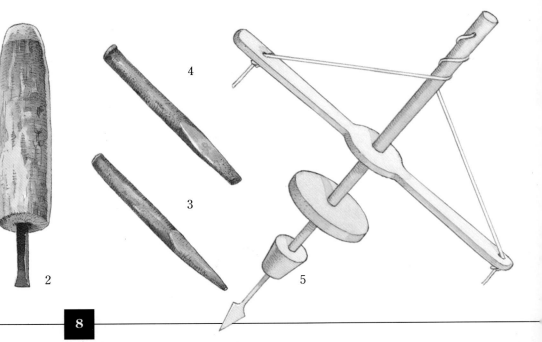

♦ TOOLS
1. A wooden maul showing obvious signs of use;
2. A wooden-handled bronze punch;
3. & 4. Bronze chisels;
5. A bow-shaped drill.

THE KING'S ARCHERS ♦
From the palace of
Artaxerxes at Susa
(Iran), 4th century BC
(Louvre, Paris). The
bricks were made in
molds, enameled,
and assembled into
large compositions.

♦ METALS
Once people began to
learn how to make
metals, they were able
to produce tools
suitable for working
on various materials.
Copper was known in
Egypt as early as 5000
BC. It became known
in the Mediterranean
between 4000 and
3000 BC and in
Europe in 2000 BC.
Copper was not hard
enough for working
on stone, but an alloy
of copper and tin was
much more resistant:
bronze. With
instruments made of
bronze it became
possible to carve
softer stone and wear
down harder stone.
Another metal, iron,
was even more
resistant. It became
widely used after
about 500 BC, and so
it was around then
that sculptors began
to work with
iron tools.

♦ A MOLD
An ancient mold for
making bricks.

WINGED GUARDIAN ♦
(Louvre, Paris) In the
ancient Assyrian
capital of Nimrud,
883-859 BC, the doors
to the palace of King
Asurnasirpal II were
guarded by two
gigantic winged bulls
with human heads.
Over 3 meters
(10 feet) tall, these
creatures with their
bodies in relief and
their heads fully
rounded were
designed to be
viewed from the front
and from the side.
The sculptor gave the
creature two legs
seen from the front
and four legs seen
from the side. In
total, therefore, it has
five legs.

♦ CLAY
Mesopotamia had
very little stone but
an abundance of clay.
Builders and
sculptors used baked
and unbaked bricks.

♦ KING IDRIMI
(British Museum,
London) The Syrian
king from 1400 BC is
shown seated, front
view only. The statue,
which was made from
a marble cube
slightly rounded off at
the corners, is
completely out of
proportion. All
attention is focused
on the face, with its
large, staring eyes.

SCULPTING MOUNTAINS

The huge size of ancient Egyptian monuments is one of the most extraordinary aspects of the art of this civilization. The Egyptians managed to raise enormous pyramids and carve out the walls of mountains. In ancient Egypt, art was a political instrument used to describe the power of the pharaoh. The message of a work of art had to be clear: everyone from scribes to peasants had to understand at first glance that the great image of the pharaoh was a sign of his limitless power. The message was conveyed not just by the statue's size, but also by the solemn pose in which the pharaoh was shown and the way in which his features were simplified. Statues of court dignitaries, on the other hand, showed their actual physical characteristics, and common people were always portrayed at work. Artists had to follow a code, so that their pictures and statues clearly reflected the strict hierarchy of ancient Egyptian society.

✦ ABU SIMBEL
Built by order of Pharaoh Rameses II (1290-1224 BC), the complex of Abu Simbel was dug out of a slope on the banks of the Nile. On the front of the largest temple, 30 meters (100 feet) high and 40 meters (130 feet) wide, there are four colossal images of the pharaoh and countless small statues and bas-reliefs telling the story of his deeds. When the Aswan Dam was constructed, the whole complex was moved, to preserve it from the river water. It took from 1963 to 1972 to dismantle and reassemble its 1,036 pieces.

✦ A SCRAPER
The Egyptians used a copper tool like this for rubbing down the surface of the sculpture before painting it.

STONEMASONS ✦
Stonemasons transformed the slope into a series of high steps, and took the enormous stones down, for constructing buildings.

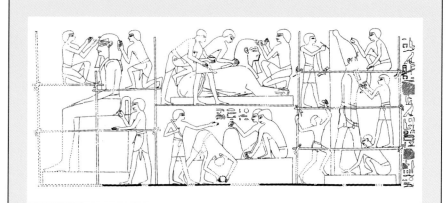

✦ SCULPTORS AT WORK
In the tomb of the vizir Rekhmira, there is a painting of a sculptor's workshop. It shows various stages in the creation of a sculpture, with each worker intent on his own particular task.
On the left, one sculptor uses a small chisel to work on a colossal seated statue, while his companions carry out the finishing touches by rubbing it down with abrasive stones.
In the center, two sculptors use a chisel and a scraper to work on a sphinx, and a third approaches holding a spatula. Below, other workers are occupied with the finishing off.
In the right-hand section, there is a clear view of a painter, holding an ink-pot in his left hand and a long paint-brush in his right hand. He is drawing the outline of a large standing statue.

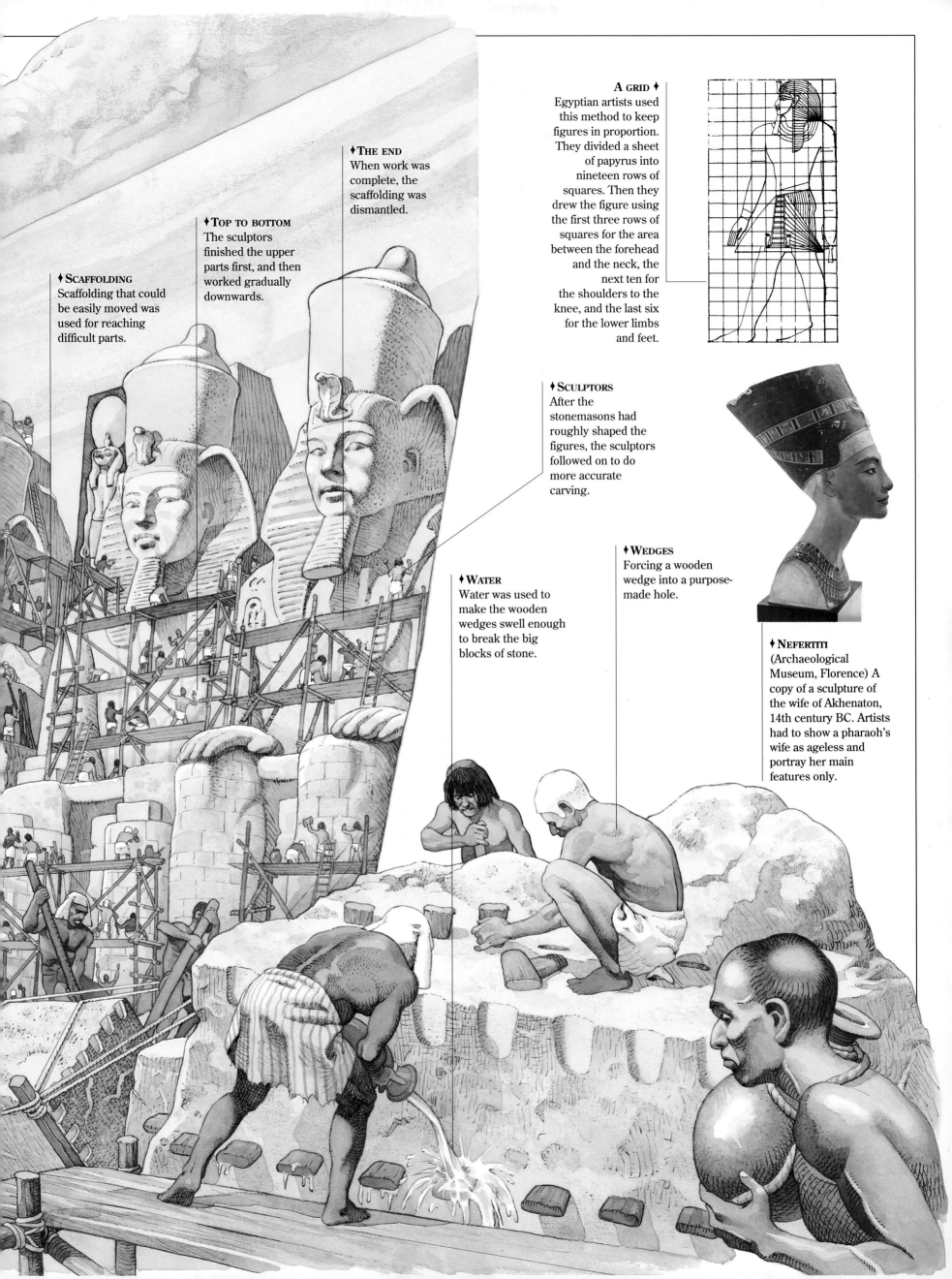

♦ **SCAFFOLDING**
Scaffolding that could be easily moved was used for reaching difficult parts.

♦ **TOP TO BOTTOM**
The sculptors finished the upper parts first, and then worked gradually downwards.

♦ **THE END**
When work was complete, the scaffolding was dismantled.

♦ **A GRID**
Egyptian artists used this method to keep figures in proportion. They divided a sheet of papyrus into nineteen rows of squares. Then they drew the figure using the first three rows of squares for the area between the forehead and the neck, the next ten for the shoulders to the knee, and the last six for the lower limbs and feet.

♦ **SCULPTORS**
After the stonemasons had roughly shaped the figures, the sculptors followed on to do more accurate carving.

♦ **WATER**
Water was used to make the wooden wedges swell enough to break the big blocks of stone.

♦ **WEDGES**
Forcing a wooden wedge into a purpose-made hole.

♦ **NEFERTITI**
(Archaeological Museum, Florence) A copy of a sculpture of the wife of Akhenaton, 14th century BC. Artists had to show a pharaoh's wife as ageless and portray her main features only.

SCULPTORS AND ARCHITECTS

Sculpture and architecture are inseparable in classical Greek art. For example, it is impossible to think of a Greek temple without the sculpted figures that decorate it. Even though the sculpture completed the building, it remained secondary to the architecture of the building itself. The shapes of the spaces within which sculptors had to place their figures affected the way in which they portrayed their subjects. For instance, sculptures of figures engaged in battle had to be enclosed within the triangular shape of a pediment, at the front of a building. The sculptor was also restricted in the subject matter that could be shown. The sculpture had to be connected with the god or goddess to whom the temple was dedicated; and it had to be in line with the wishes of the person who had commissioned the temple to be built. The Greeks celebrated and commemorated real-life events by making sculptures of mythological characters and stories. In this way they were different from the Romans, whose sculpture represented actual events.

A CENTAUR ✦
A metope from the Parthenon (British Museum, London). In Greek mythology, centaurs were a tribe of strange beings, half man and half horse. One story tells of the Greek hero Theseus helping to defeat the centaurs in a battle, and many artists have represented this.

✦THE PEDIMENT
To fill the triangular space of the pediment with figures which were in proportion to each other, the Greek sculptor composed a scene where the figures at the sides were either kneeling or lying down.

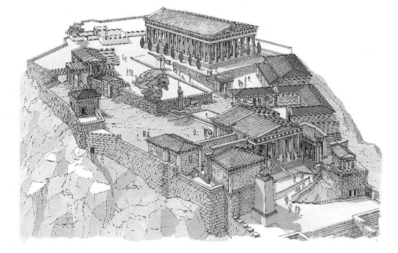

♦PHIDIAS AND THE PARTHENON
The temple to Athena Parthenos (the Maiden), on the Acropolis in Athens, was the idea of Pericles, who led the city-state in the 5th century BC. He ordered the temple to be built, under the supervision of Phidias, and the work was carried out between 447 and 438 BC. The two pediments contain scenes depicting stories of the goddess Athena. The frieze shows a procession and religious ceremonies held in her honor. And battle scenes on the metopes are a reference to real-life victories of Athens.

METOPES ✦
Ninety-two metopes (square panels) with mythological scenes decorate the frieze along the sides of the building.

COLUMNS ✦
The columns of the Parthenon, like those of most Greek temples, were constructed by fixing together a series of cylindrical pieces.

METAL PINS ✦
The pieces were joined with great precision, by means of metal pins through their centers. This ensured that the column was stable.

FIGURES ✦
For the first time, the figures carved in relief on the pediment protruded fully from the background.

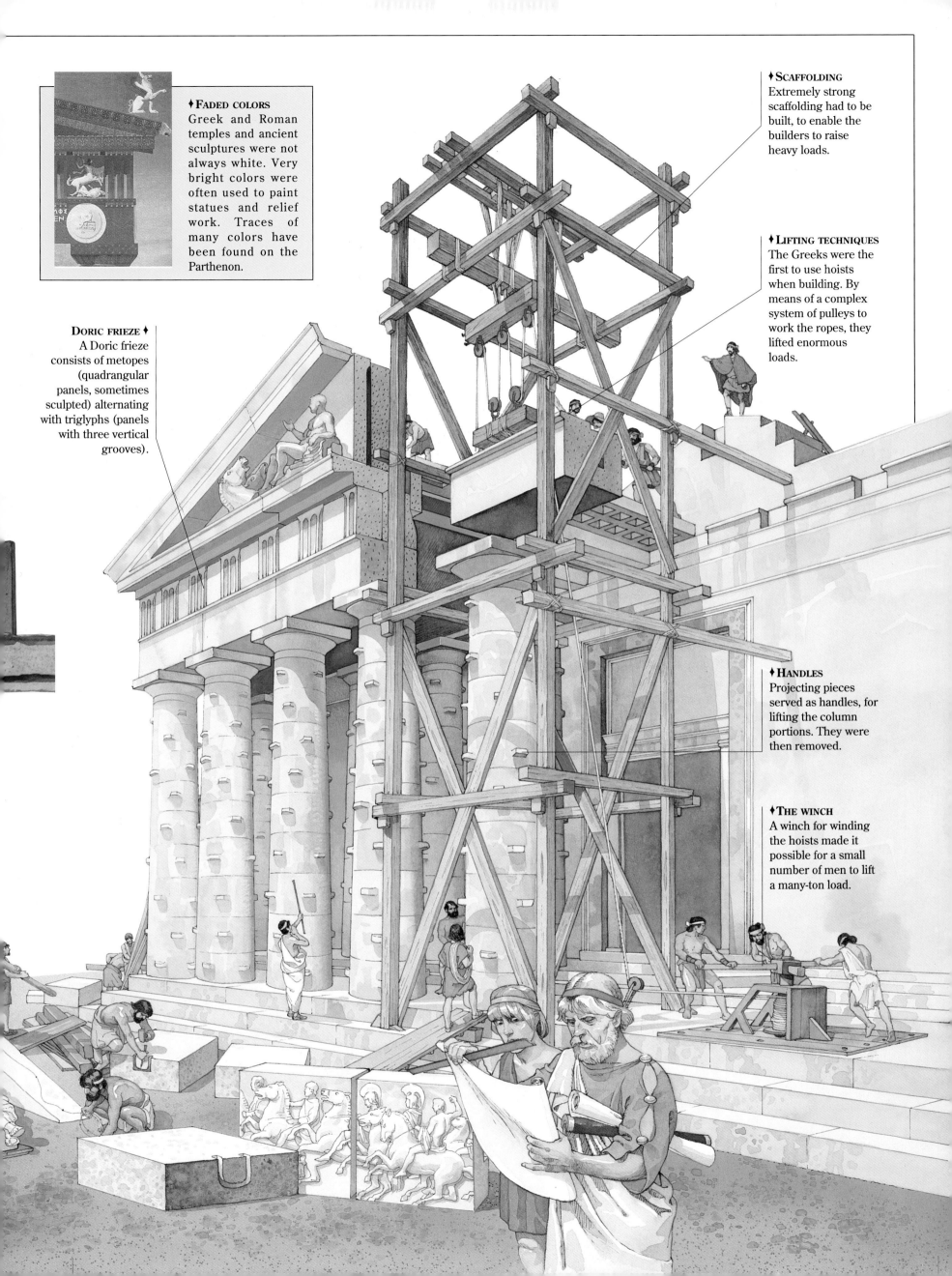

♦ **FADED COLORS**
Greek and Roman temples and ancient sculptures were not always white. Very bright colors were often used to paint statues and relief work. Traces of many colors have been found on the Parthenon.

♦ **SCAFFOLDING**
Extremely strong scaffolding had to be built, to enable the builders to raise heavy loads.

♦ **LIFTING TECHNIQUES**
The Greeks were the first to use hoists when building. By means of a complex system of pulleys to work the ropes, they lifted enormous loads.

DORIC FRIEZE ♦
A Doric frieze consists of metopes (quadrangular panels, sometimes sculpted) alternating with triglyphs (panels with three vertical grooves).

♦ **HANDLES**
Projecting pieces served as handles, for lifting the column portions. They were then removed.

♦ **THE WINCH**
A winch for winding the hoists made it possible for a small number of men to lift a many-ton load.

CASTING

Many sculptors have chosen to work in metal. From 3000 to 500 BC most artists used a primitive method: they hammered sheets of metal into shape. However, the technique of casting – melting metal and pouring it into molds – was known in Persia (now Iran) and Mesopotamia as early as 4000 BC, and this spread to Greece towards the end of the 7th century BC. At this point it was only possible to make small statues by casting. Later the technique was developed, enabling sculptors to make statues of monumental size. By the mid-5th century BC, Greek artists had learned how to retain the basic model and use it to mass-produce statues. This became the great age of the bronze statue. After the fall of the Roman Empire, the complicated and laborious technique of bronze casting was rarely used until the late Middle Ages.

♦ RIACE BRONZES
Above: the head of one of two bronze figures found in the sea near Riace, southern Italy, in 1972 (Museo Nazionale, Reggio di Calabria). Each figure was armed with a shield and a spear and expressed great physical strength. The figures were created in the mid-5th century BC, for a temple sanctuary.

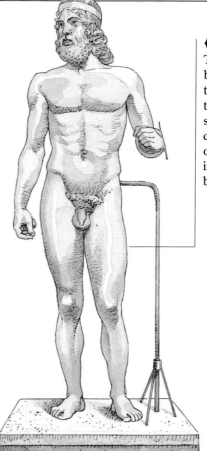

♦ 1. THE MODEL
The casting process began with making the model. This was the original design stage. The artist used clay to mold a statue of the size and shape intended for the final bronze work.

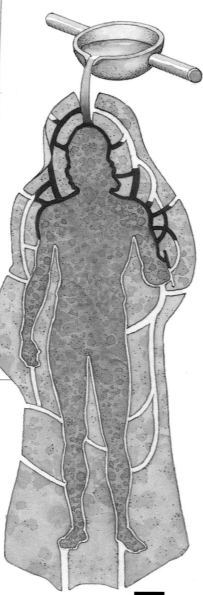

5. THE WAX MODEL ♦
The earth filling dried and then the blocks were removed to expose the wax-coated model.

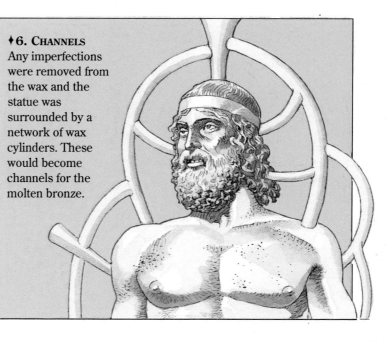

♦ 6. CHANNELS
Any imperfections were removed from the wax and the statue was surrounded by a network of wax cylinders. These would become channels for the molten bronze.

9. POURING THE ♦ METAL INTO THE CAST
The cast was placed in a pit filled with sand and wet earth. Only the head was allowed to protrude. Then bronze, melted at a temperature of over 2000° Fahrenheit, was poured into the cast, via the upper vents, to fill the whole space left by the wax. Bronze is an alloy of copper and tin, with a small amount of lead.

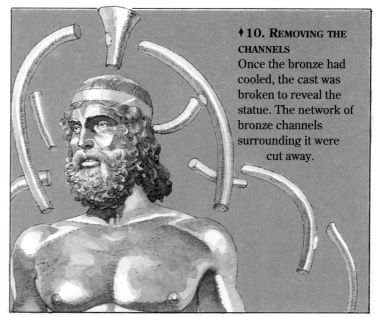

♦ 10. REMOVING THE CHANNELS
Once the bronze had cooled, the cast was broken to reveal the statue. The network of bronze channels surrounding it were cut away.

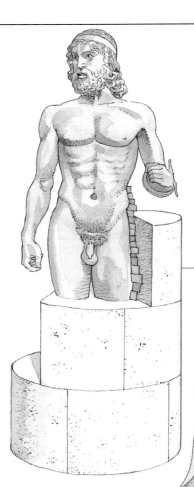

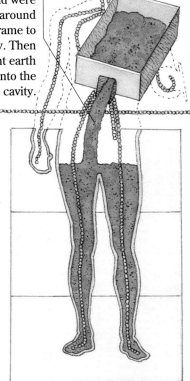

♦ 2. THE MOLD
The mold is like a negative of the model. It was made by molding blocks of plaster around the model. The mold was divided into sections, as this made it possible to take it apart and put it together again.

3. A WAX LAYER ♦
The imprint of the model inside the mold was coated with wax. The thickness of the wax would be the thickness of the bronze.

4. EARTH FILLING ♦
The sections of the mold were reassembled around an iron frame to make it sturdy. Then fire-resistant earth was poured into the cavity.

7. THE CAST ♦
To make the cast, the statue and channels were covered with a thick layer of plaster, ground-up bricks, sand and cow dung, but vents were left for the channels. The cast was to be heated, so strong metal bands were fastened around it, to prevent it breaking in the fire.

Air vents.

♦ 8. LOST WAX
The cast was heated to a temperature of 400°-575° Fahrenheit. This caused the wax to melt and pour out through the vents, leaving a space. At 1100° F, the cast was baked.

Metal bands to strengthen the cast.

The melted wax pours out of the cast.

♦ 11. FINISHING
The surface of the statue was cleaned to remove any defects and the earth filling was taken away through the base.

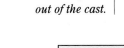

♦ 12. DETAILS
The sculptor added the final details, such as the eyes. Eyelashes and eyebrows were engraved and the irises were painted on. Sometimes semi-precious stones or shells were used to make the pupils shine.

♦ LOST AND FOUND
How did the Riace bronzes, two large ancient Greek statues, come to be on the bed of the Ionian Sea, off southern Italy? The ancient Romans loved Greek art. They collected works by the ancient masters and took them to Rome. Most probably, the two statues were being transported to Rome along the Ionian route and were part of a shipwreck. They were discovered on 16 August 1972 when the arm of one of the statues was noticed emerging from the sandy sea-bed.

Greek Statues

In the 5th and the 4th centuries BC, Greek artists developed the portrayal of the human figure. The idea was already established that statues should show how the human body works. The new statues were based on an ideal of perfection and beauty which the sculptors achieved by following carefully worked-out mathematical rules. The figures were therefore balanced and symmetrical and in proportion, as real-life human figures are not. And yet, as time went on, the Greek sculptors also made their ideally beautiful figures look increasingly natural. Works by Myron, Polyclitus, Praxiteles and Lysippus present fine human figures in marble and bronze: twenty-year-olds with athletic bodies and men and women with perfect features and expressions of calm serenity. Most of the original Greek statues have been lost, but the Romans made many copies of them and these do remain. Some people think that the marble statue of *Hermes and the Infant Dionysus* found at Olympia is the original by Praxiteles.

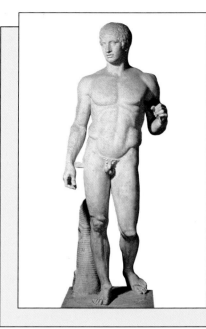

♦ **THE DORYPHORUS**
A Roman copy of a statue by Polyclitus, called the *Doryphorus* (spear carrier) (Museo Archeologico, Naples). Polyclitus was not just portraying an athlete. The figure showed what the sculptor believed to be the ideal of male beauty, according to rules about proportion that he had worked out. For example, the head is exactly one-sixth of the size of the whole body.

♦ THE GODS

Greek sculptors made no distinction between portraying gods and portraying men. *Hermes* and *Apollo*, by Praxiteles, seem like two athletes resting after a victory. *Zeus* might almost be a javelin thrower. All the figures express the ideal of perfection and beauty.

1. Praxiteles, *Hermes and the Infant Dionysus*, 4th century BC, Roman copy (Olympia);
2. Praxiteles, *Apollo*, Roman copy (Louvre, Paris);
3. *Zeus* or *Poseidon*, 460 BC (National Museum, Athens).

1

2

3

Greek sculptors chose
mostly male subjects
when portraying
humans. They used
female figures more
for statues of deities
and to represent
qualities such as
Peace or Victory. Male
statues were always
nude. Female statues
were of figures clothed
in wet-looking
drapery, which still
showed the anatomy.
The Greeks did not
portray female nudes
until the mid-5th
century BC.

1. *Venus of Fréjus*, a
Roman copy of a work
attributed to
Callimachus (Louvre,
Paris);
2. *Eirene holding the
Infant Pluto*, a Roman
copy of a work by
Cephisodotus
(Antikensammlungen,
Munich);
3. *Aphrodite of Cnidus*
by Praxiteles (Musei
Vaticani, Rome).

✦ MEN

In ancient Greece,
winners of gymnastic
games and heroes in
battle were seen as
people whom the
gods had greatly
favored. Statues of
these people would
be made and
presented to a
temple, as a way of
giving thanks to the
gods for their victory.
Athletes and warriors
both stood for valor,
fighting with courage

for a noble cause.
They were worthy of
being portrayed like
mythological gods.

1. Myron, *The Discus
Thrower*, a Roman
copy (Musei Vaticani,
Rome);
2. *Wounded Warrior*,
from the Temple of
Aegina, early 5th
century BC
(Antikensammlungen,
Munich).

THE ROMANS

The greatness of the Roman Empire is reflected in the fact that Roman times are such a well-known period of ancient history. This is partly because so many of the great buildings constructed by the Romans still remain. Many monuments were erected to honor or give thanks for a victory, and low-relief sculptures on these monuments illustrate the emperors, public events and victorious exploits. The sculpting of so-called historic reliefs was most widespread during the Imperial age, from the end of the 1st century BC. Ordering public works and monuments was a way for an emperor to emphasize his political decisions and show off his greatness. His aim was to prove that his actions were more admirable than those of his predecessors. Historic reliefs, faithfully portraying sequences of events, can be found on triumphal arches, decorated columns, such as Trajan's column in Rome, and public buildings. They tell part of the story of the Roman people.

♦ **TRAJAN'S COLUMN**
Inaugurated in AD 113, the column was designed to hold the remains of Emperor Trajan (98-117) and to commemorate the building of the forum which he ordered. A frieze, over 300 meters (985 feet) long, wraps around the column twenty-three times. It tells the story of Trajan's victories over the Dacians, the ancient people of what is now Romania. They were defeated in 101 and 102 and finally subjugated during 105 and 106. The scenes on the frieze, in which the emperor is almost always present, appear in chronological order, like frames in a cartoon strip. Trajan is shown with the Roman army crossing the river Danube, and in scenes of battle and of life in the army camp. He is seen preparing battle plans, at the head of his troops, with ambassadors and with the vanquished. In all, he appears fifty-eight times.

♦ **DROWNING**
This scene from the frieze on Trajan's column illustrates an episode that occurred during the first Dacian war. During a battle fought on a frozen river, the ice gave way and the Dacian cavalry drowned. The mounted soldiers are shown clinging desperately to their horses, while their companions on the river bank are trying to help them.

♦ **THE ARMY**
Soldiers carry their legion's banners and standards. One is leading a bull, which is to be offered as a sacrifice.

♦ **THE BRIDGE**
Behind is the bridge over the Danube built by Apollodorus of Damascus, the designer also of Trajan's forum. Built of wood and supported on stone pylons, the bridge was a marvelous work of engineering.

♦ **TRAJAN**
Trajan makes the sacrifice. There are offerings on the altar and the bull on the left is also to be offered to the god.

♦ **Scaffolding**
Enormous wooden scaffolding was constructed so that the huge portions of the column, over 3.5 meters (11.5 feet) in diameter, could be lifted and mounted with precision.

♦ **Hoists**
Four large hoists, which were used to position the column portions, were attached to the top of the scaffolding.

♦ **The libraries**
Beside the column were twin libraries, from which the sculpted scenes could be admired from different levels.

♦ **Winches**
Each hoist was operated from the ground by a horizontal winch turned by a team of workmen.

♦ **Sacrifice**
This medallion, showing a sacrifice, was part of one of Hadrian's (AD 117-138) monuments, re-used in the *Arch of Constantine*, Rome, AD 313. By making public sacrifices, emperors demonstrated their devotion to the gods.

♦ **In charge**
A team leader gave orders for the ropes to be alternately tightened and slackened.

♦ **Internal stairs**
A spiral staircase was carved inside the column portions, to give access to the top.

Judging ♦
This relief from a triumphal arch of Marcus Aurelius, AD 180, was also used on the *Arch of Constantine*. It shows the emperor judging prisoners.

MAKING PORTRAITS

The Romans used to carry wax images of their ancestors in funeral processions, and wealthy families took pride in displaying busts of their ancestors at home. In the Republican age, from the 2nd century BC, it was more common among broader bands of the population to have portraits made of family members. Also, busts and statues were made to honor people who had performed valiant deeds for the state. Portraits became most popular during the Imperial age, between the 1st and the 3rd centuries AD. Emperors would have busts of themselves made, expressing qualities such as justice and valor. The busts were meant to reflect something of the life, work and commitment to civic and political duty of the person portrayed. They captured personality because they concentrated on facial features. To a large extent, busts took the place of statues of the whole body, as used by the Greeks, and statues of athletes, so highly favored by the Greeks, were completely abandoned.

1

2

3

✦ ANCESTORS

A funerary portrait was made as soon as someone died, using a death mask. This was a wax mold placed over the person's face, so as to make a cast of his or her features. Some people underwent this unpleasant procedure while they were still alive so that a more faithful image of them could be handed down.

1. *Head* from the tomb of the Valerii (Musei Vaticani, Rome;
2. *Shoemaker*, late 1st century AD (Musei Capitolini, Rome);
3. *Patrician with Busts of Ancestors*, early 1st century AD (Palazzo dei Conservatori, Rome).

3

✦ VETERANS

In the Republican age, public portraits were dedicated to triumvirs and magistrates. Moral qualities are expressed through deeply lined faces.

1. *Julius Caesar*, mid-1st century BC (Museo Barracco, Rome); 2. *Sulla*, 75 BC (Museo Archeologico, Venice); 3. *Brutus*, 3rd century BC (Musei Capitolini, Rome).

1

2

3

4

✦ COINS

Roman rulers were depicted on coins, a sign of their power and wealth. The side-view portrait became the typical style used on coins worldwide for thousands of years afterwards.

1. *Julius Caesar*, denarius, 43 BC (Museo civico archeologico, Bologna);
2. *Brutus*, gold coin, 42 BC (Münzkabinett, Berlin);
3. *Mark Antony*, gold coin, 39 BC (Münzkabinett, Berlin);
4. *Octavian*, gold coin, 29 BC (Münzkabinett, Berlin).

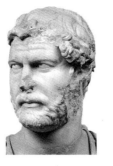

1

2

3

4

✦ EMPERORS

It gave an emperor prestige to be portrayed as a god. Claudius, crippled and old, was portrayed as a handsome Jupiter. A bust of Hadrian showed him with the thoughtful face of a philosopher. Caracalla was given the fierce expression of a terrible despot. Funerary portraits, for more private use, were more true likenesses.

1. *Hadrian*, AD 117-138 (Louvre, Paris);
2. *Caracalla*, early 3rd century AD (Palazzo dei Conservatori, Rome);
3. *Vespasian*, AD 69-70 (Musei Capitolini, Rome);
4. *Trajan*, AD c.117 (Archaeological Museum, Ankara);
5. *Claudius*, mid-1st century AD (Musei Vaticani, Rome).

5

1

2

✦ THE FAMILY

Portraits of women and children give an impression of Roman daily life. The matron, with a hairstyle to enhance her beauty, wears sumptuous clothes. Other portraits suggest domestic tranquillity.

1. *Mother and Daughter*, late 1st century BC (Musei Capitolini, Rome);
2. *Portrait*, late 1st century AD (Musei Capitolini, Rome);
3. *Young girl*, 1st century BC (Museo Nazionale Romano, Rome);
4. *Matron*, 1st century AD (Louvre, Paris).

3

4

ANCIENT CHINA

From about 1500 BC, the Yellow River area of China was ruled by the Shang, one of the first of a series of dynasties, including the Han, Sung and Tang, which made their mark on the country's history. The Chinese discovered how to make paper, silk and porcelain and how to print, and such inventions affected Chinese art. Painting and calligraphy are more representative of Chinese art than sculpture. Chinese architecture did not allow for sculptured decoration, and there was little demand for statues, except in connection with Buddhism, which came to China during the Han dynasty (206 BC-AD 220). Chinese sculpture consists mostly of small objects: vessels cast from bronze, from 1000 BC, funerary statuettes, pottery and porcelain. However, there is an outstanding Chinese example of life-size terracotta statues: the *Xian Warriors*, thousands of figures set to defend the underground tomb of Qin Shi Huangdi, the first emperor of China, who ruled from 221 to 210 BC.

♦A BURIED ARMY
In 1974, while digging a well for water, a group of peasants from the village of Xian unearthed some terracotta statues. This proved to be one of the greatest archaeological discoveries of the 20th century. More than 8,000 statues, standing ready for battle, in orderly ranks, had been buried in long ditches. Each life-size general, foot-soldier, archer and horse was different from the rest, with individual features. For over 2,000 years, the great terracotta army had stood guard over the "room of sleep" where the fierce Qin Shi Huangdi had been buried in 210 BC.

BRONZE WORK ♦
A ritual vessel for use in a temple, 12th century BC (Musée Cernuschi, Paris). At this early date the Chinese were skilled in bronze casting.

♦AN ARCHER
From the Museum of the Tomb of Qin Shi Huangdi, Lintong, Shaanxi province.

SUPERVISION ♦
A supervisor kept a careful eye on all the workers.

BEAMS ♦
Strong beams would support the weight of the earth.

HEADS ♦
A workman delivers the warriors' heads. These would be fixed carefully to the figures once they were in position.

♦A TANG FIGURE
This brightly colored glazed terracotta figure from the mid-8th century looks like delicate porcelain (Art Institute, Chicago).

A HAN LAMP ♦
Late 2nd century. Smoke was channeled away through the hollow right arm of the lady. Art and craftsmanship together created an object both beautiful and functional (Metropolitan Museum of Art, New York).

A SUNG BODHISATTVA ♦
A painted wood figure from AD 950. In Buddhism, a bodhisattva is a compassionate being who has gained enlightenment but stays on earth to help other people gain enlightenment too (Staatliche Museum Berlin).

♦COVERING
A covering made from planks.

♦IN POSITION
The figures without their heads were lowered into position in the graves. The heads were attached later.

♦MATTING
Before everything was covered with earth, straw matting was laid over the beams to provide further protection.

♦PAINTING
Once everything was in place, work began on painting the statues.

INDIAN SCULPTURE

For thousands of years Indian art has been linked closely to the religions that developed in this civilization. Sculptors have produced work ranging from small figures of deities to monumental statues and temples, sometimes carved out of rocky slopes, and covered with sculpted figures. According to Hindu and Buddhist thinking, everything we perceive in this world is only outward show. People should try not to become too attached to material things, but instead seek to be reunited with God. Works of art are seen as intermediaries between humans and the gods. When picturing the gods, artists are expected to follow tradition, using familiar symbols and showing their subjects in recognized poses. Large numbers of bronze statues of the Hindu deity Shiva Nataraja – Dancing Shiva – have been made, like the one shown here. The sculptor has incorporated many traditional symbols into the work but still created something fresh and natural.

♦ **SHIVA NATARAJA**
A traditional figure from the 19th-20th century (Oriental Museum, Durham University).

RHYTHM ♦
The small drum in Shiva's hand beats out the rhythm of the creative dance.

♦ **EARTH SPIRIT**
A "yakshi" (earth spirit), 1.6 meters (5.25 feet) high, sculpted in sandstone in the Mauryan period, c.200 BC (Patna Museum, Patna). The smooth, shiny skin contrasts with the detailed carving of clothes and the fan she carries.

BUDDHA ♦
A 5th-century Gupta sandstone sculpture of the Buddha preaching his first sermon, in the deer park at Sarnath (Archaeological Museum, Sarnath). 1.6 meters (5.25 feet) high. The panel below includes two deer.

CREATION AND ♦
DESTRUCTION
The circle represents the universe, which Shiva creates, and the flames his destruction of it.

DEMON OF ♦
IGNORANCE
Shiva stamps on the demon of ignorance.

♦ **THE SANCHI STUPA**
A stupa is a burial mound containing relics of the Buddha. The stupa at Sanchi was built in the 2nd century BC. Four carved stone gates, 10.4 meters (34 feet) high, were added in the late 1st century BC and early 1st century AD.

♦ **CENTERS OF ART**
Some of the most important centers of ancient Indian art.

LION CAPITAL ♦
The emperor Ashoka, who ruled from 273 to 232 BC, had many columns erected, to mark important Buddhist places. This polished stone lion is from the top of one of them (Archaeological Museum, Sarnath).

CLASSICAL DRAPERY ♦
Roman traders passed through Gandhara, in the north-west of India. The influence of classical sculpture shows clearly in the clothing of this Gandharan statue from the 4th-5th centuries (National Museum, Kabul).

♦ **MALE FACE**
The oldest examples of sculpture from India date back to the Indus Valley civilization which flourished in northern India from c.2300 to 1750 BC. (National Museum, New Delhi).

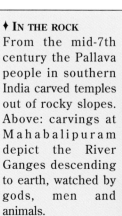

♦ **SHIVA**
The Hindu god Shiva destroys and recreates the universe. The image of him as Lord of the Dance represents these contradictory aspects and includes many other symbols.

♦ **IN THE ROCK**
From the mid-7th century the Pallava people in southern India carved temples out of rocky slopes.
Above: carvings at Mahabalipuram depict the River Ganges descending to earth, watched by gods, men and animals.
Below: Kailasantha Temple at Ellura, 8th century, was thought of as a copy of Mount Kailasa, Shiva's dwelling place in the Himalayas.

ROMANESQUE SCULPTURE

The main door to a Romanesque church is an imposing sight with its richly sculptured tympanum (the area between the top of the door and the arch). For centuries, sculpture on churches had been banned, for fear that worshipers would mistake the statues for images of ancient pagan gods. Then, towards the end of the 11th century, the Catholic Church rediscovered the power of carvings to capture people's attention. Scenes that Romanesque artists carved around church doors were designed to attract attention and to teach people about Christian beliefs. Worshipers entering the church to take part in a service saw images around the doorway representing Good and Evil, Salvation and Damnation. These were intended as reminders of the need to repent and make atonement for your sins in order to enter the Kingdom of God. The path followed into the church was a symbol of the soul's journey through life.

PISCES ✦
Signs of the zodiac and farming scenes are carved in circular frames in the arch. Daily activities and religion were intermingled.

HEAVEN ✦
Mary and the apostles are portrayed to the right of Christ among hosts of angels. Next to them, souls of the blessed are ascending into heaven.

THE CHOSEN ✦
The souls of the just rise out of their graves, propelled towards heaven by angelic creatures.

ST MICHAEL ✦
St Michael, sword in hand, separates the souls of the chosen from those of the damned.

✦ AT THE DOOR
As they arrive, worshipers and pilgrims pause to look at the carved images.

✦ THE LAST JUDGEMENT
The tympanum over the west door of Saint-Lazare, Autun, was carved by Gislebertus, who worked on the church from 1120 to 1135. It is made of twenty-nine blocks of stone, carved and then put together. Gislebertus put his name at the bottom, under the feet of Christ.

♦ HARVEST
An image of a farmer treading grapes in a large vat represents the work done at harvest time, during the month of September.

♦ JESUS CHRIST
Christ is shown sitting on the heavenly throne surrounded by light. He holds out his palms to show the stigmata, the marks left by the nails which were used to hang him on the cross.

♦ WEIGHING SOULS
There are two souls to be judged, on the dishes of the scales held by the Archangel Michael. A creature from hell clutches on the wicked side because judgement is in favor of the good.

♦ THE DAMNED
The dead leave their graves and the souls of the damned are dragged down to hell by great skeleton hands that look like pincers.

Apostle, Saint-Sernin, Toulouse, c.1100.

♦ ORIGINS
The first examples of Romanesque art appeared to the north and south of the Pyrenees during the late 11th and early 12th centuries. At the church of Saint-Sernin in Toulouse there are fabulous sculptures around the doors, at the altar table and on the capitals of pillars. A few decades later, the *de Francia* and *de las Platerías* doors embellished the cathedral of Compostela.

David, Santiago de Compostela, c.1100.

The spread of Romanesque architecture was helped by two factors. The Cluniac Order of monks and nuns, founded in France, expanded and built abbeys in the new style throughout Europe. And people traveling as pilgrims spread ideas from country to country.

PILGRIMS' WEAR ♦
The pilgrims wore broad-brimmed hats to shade them from the sun, held walking-sticks to help them on the long march and carried knapsacks over their shoulders. A shell was stitched to the hat or cloak. This was the symbol of pilgrims going to Santiago de Compostela.

PILGRIMS ♦
Between the 10th and the 13th centuries, thousands of faithful Christians traveled from one end of Europe to the other to visit holy places. Churches, abbeys and cathedrals were built along the great pilgrim routes that led to Rome in Italy and Santiago de Compostela in Spain.

Music, from the deambulatory of Cluny Abbey, c.1115, demolished in the 18th-19th centuries (Cluny Museum).

CHARTRES

A burst of urban development took place in Europe during the 12th and 13th centuries. City walls were extended and churches, public buildings, bridges, roads and houses were built. A new style of architecture arose in the Ile-de-France and spread to towns around centers of pilgrimage and along the roads between them. The style, called Gothic, is characterized by pointed arches, flying buttresses and tall windows. Great Gothic cathedrals, as at Chartres, were adorned with impressive sculptures. A cathedral building site would be feverishly busy, sometimes for a whole century. The Master of Works was the architect in charge, and all the sculptors answered to him. He was an expert in stone-cutting, which was the basis for cross-vault construction, and also deeply knowledgeable about sculpture. He would watch the stone-cutters, the stone-dressers, who carried out the ornamental work, and the sculptors, as they made the column-like statues to decorate the doorways.

✦ CHARTRES
The cathedral was built in 1144-55 in the early Gothic style, but a fire in 1194 destroyed all but the towers and the west face. The rest was rebuilt in the 13th century and it was consecrated in 1260.

✦ STONE FACING
Slender pillars placed close together on the walls by the doorway were decorated with botanic and geometric designs. These made a background for the statue columns.

✦ LION OF ST MARK
The symbols of the gospel writers surround the figure of Christ in the central tympanum.

MASTER OF WORKS ✦
He supervised the sculptors. Often, responsibility for the whole construction site was given to a sculptor who also acted as architect.

WORKING METHOD ✦
The stones were propped up in an almost horizontal position and the sculptors completed the statues there, before they were placed on the façade.

✦ CLOTHING
The stone was so finely carved that the fabric of clothing looked extraordinarily realistic.

STATUE COLUMNS ✦
The figure and the column were carved from a single block of stone. Having chosen the piece, the artists tried to adapt the figure to the stone's natural shape. The pose might vary only slightly, in the angle of an arm or the way in which an object was represented.

♦ **MOUNTING**
The finished statue columns were hoisted onto the walls by means of strong winches.

♦ **MEASURING**
The measurements of the blocks were checked. The building was designed according to mathematical rules.

LINTELS ♦
The stone blocks which would support the arch of the tympanum were carved with figures of the apostles, grouped in threes.

♦ **A GOTHIC CONSTRUCTION SITE**
A 15th-century miniature of *The Building of the Temple of Jerusalem*, by Jean Fouquet (Bibliothèque Nationale, Paris).
Some of the workers square blocks of stone, while a sculptor is intent on carving a statue.

♦ **FINISHING OFF**
Final delicate detail was added to the sculpture after it had been mounted on the wall.

♦ *Three figures*, a detail of the statue columns to the left of the west door of Chartres Cathedral.

GOTHIC SCULPTURE

Towards the middle of the 12th century, for the first time since the end of the classical (Greek and Roman) period, a new type of monumental sculpture appeared: great column-like statues on the façades of imposing cathedrals. Early examples of these figures flanking cathedral doorways are rigid. They are not easily distinguishable from the columns from which they were carved. The heads face forwards, the eyes stare, the arms hang by the figures' sides and their garments hang in straight, parallel folds. Examples from only fifty years later are more rounded and better-proportioned. The figures became more life-like and stood out from the background in more natural poses. As Gothic sculpture gradually became more realistic, there was a return to completely rounded statuary. Early 14th-century statues were of figures dressed in soft drapery, through which the contours of the body could be seen. They resembled statues of the classical age, with their natural poses and harmonious proportions.

♦ SAINTS
Chartres Cathedral, portico of the west face, 1145-55. The figures are rigid, enclosed within a limited space, and seem to be held back by the material from which they are made. With staring, expressionless eyes, each figure is isolated within its own block of stone, and there is no sense that one relates to the next.

♦ SILVER AND GOLD
Gothic sculpture does not consist only of religious statues and sculptures on cathedral façades. There are smaller objects in the Gothic style. Chalices and monstrances and gold reliquaries set with precious stones and enamel are halfway between sculpture and the goldsmith's art. Left: the Sceptre of Charles V of France, 1365-80 (Louvre, Paris).

♦ GERMANY
The Gothic style was adopted late in Germany. Cathedral façades remained in the late Romanesque style and were not fully adorned with sculpture. Gothic sculpture was used inside. The Bamburg *Knight*, c.1236, and the *Founders* in Naumburg Cathedral, c.1249, brought civilian subjects into the churches.

♦ SPAIN
In 1188 Mateo de Compostela finished the great *Portico de la Gloria* at the Cathedral of Santiago de Compostela. The numberless statues above the triple doorway represent *Universal Judgement, Christ in Judgement, Christ Descending into Limbo*. This was the beginning of Spanish Gothic.

THE VIRGIN MARY ♦ AND ST ELIZABETH Reims Cathedral, portico of the west face, pre-1260. The two figures stand well forward from the background. They are amply draped. Their cloaks, worn over their heads and falling in full, sweeping folds, are reminiscent of the clothing of classical statues. In this case, there is a clear sense that the two figures are relating to each other.

♦ ITALY Outstanding Gothic sculptors included Arnolfo di Cambio and father and son, Nicola and Giovanni Pisano. Ancient art had not been forgotten. Giovanni's *Madonna and Child* (left), Padua, 1305-6, resembles a Greek goddess, and Nicola's Pulpit for Siena Cathedral (right), 1265-68, is in classical style.

♦ ENGLAND Statues were not carved on façades that already had a lot of architectural decoration. The figures at York Minster, such as the one of *Moses* (left),

1200-10, are an exception. However, there were many statues inside, including sculpture on tombs, such as that of England's King John, 1225-35, in Worcester Cathedral.

JAPAN

During the 6th century AD Buddhism spread to Japan, first from Korea and then from China. The religion had a strong impact on Japanese sculpture. In 741, the emperor Shomu, an ardent follower of Buddhism, ordered that a monastery for men and one for women should be built in every province, at the expense of the state. The monastery of Todai-ji at Nara became the chief one of them all. It is said that the emperor had artists come from all over Asia to create a 16 meter (52 feet) high bronze statue of the Buddha at Nara; and that it used up all the country's reserves of bronze and precious metals. Japanese sculptors were influenced by those from India and China. Nonetheless, they gradually developed their own techniques and styles. For example, in the 18th century, they produced colossal statues of supernatural guardian-gods and infernal judges. These were characterized by violently angry expressions and tremendously muscular bodies which seemed to glorify men's physical strength.

♦ AN ORIENTAL METHOD
A method used for making statues in Japan was to apply layers of hempen cloth soaked in lacquer to a base made of clay, terracotta or wood. Parts of the statue such as the arms and legs were also wired. The cloth was modeled and left to dry. Finally the surface was painted or gilded.
Above: *The god Ashura*, Kofukuji, Nara, 8th century AD.

♦ INAUGURATION
In 752, thousands of monks from all corners of Japan and the rest of Asia, together with members of the court, foreign ambassadors, and army officers, came to take part in the ceremony to open the eyes of the great Buddha at Nara. Flanked by his guard, the emperor Shomu held one end of a cord, to which a paint brush was attached. An Indian monk, Bodhisena, on some high scaffolding, used the brush to paint on the irises of the statue, so instilling it with life.

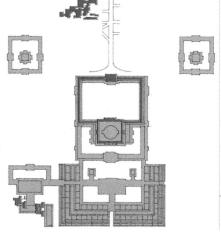

♦ THE TEMPLE OF TODAI-JI
The emperor Shomu (701-756) ordered that the great temple of Todai-ji should be built in the city of Nara, and that a huge bronze statue of the Buddha should be created there, symbolizing the alliance between Buddhism and the state. On the right, the parts of the temple which survive are shown in red. Parts destroyed by fire and pillage are shown in grey.

♦ NI-O
A figure sculpted by Unkei in 1203. It is one of two which stand guard at the doors of the Todai-ji temple in Nara. They are protectors of the Buddhist law. The figure is a bodhisattva, a being who is about to become a Buddha but who forgoes Nirvana in order to help others along their path of salvation.

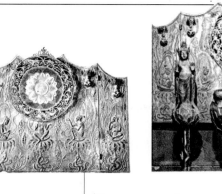

♦THE TRIAD OF AMIDA
Horui-ji, Nara. A little shrine made in the 7th century for Lady Tachibana, a member of the imperial court.

The triad of Amida, the Buddha of Infinite Light, sit on three lotus flowers rising from the surface of a pool.

♦ PREHISTORIC FIGURE
From Azuma village, prefecture of Gumma.

♦ SHAKA BUDDHA
Muro-ji, Nara. Wood was widely used for sculptures in the Heian period.

♦ SHUKONGO
Todai-ji, Nara. The god of lightning is one of Buddhism's guardian-gods. This is one of the terracotta works from the *Hokke-do* group.

After figures from prehistory like the one above, some of the most ancient Japanese sculpture is from the Asuka period (AD 538-645), when Buddhism began to spread to Japan. Often the statues were stiff-looking with severe expressions. Works from the Hakuko period (645-710) had more smiling faces like those of the *Triad* in the sanctuary of Amida. The finest example of Tempyo sculpture (710-794), the *Hokke-do* group, consists of a series of life-size terracotta statues and others, over 3 meters (10 feet) high, made with cloth soaked in lacquer. The large, painted frame of the Shaka Buddha is typical of the Heian style (794-1185). During the Kamakura period (1185-1336) images of fierce warriors appeared. Apart from the beautiful Muromachi masks (1336-1573), there was much repetition during the following periods.

♦ MASK
(Private collection) 7th century.

WORKING IN WOOD

Sculpting wood dates back to primitive times, and the technique has remained more or less unchanged for centuries. The material has advantages and limitations. Like stone, wood can only be shaped by removing material, but, unlike stone, it gives no resistance to tools and so it is easier to carve and can be worked in fine detail. The shape and size of wooden blocks are limiting factors for the sculptor, and the grain and notches in the wood are obstacles to be overcome. Wood is a living material, sensitive to atmospheric change. It contracts with heat and expands with humidity. It seasons with age and changes color when exposed to light. It is subject to mold and woodworm and deteriorates easily. Wood has been considered an inferior material, and wooden sculptures have often been painted, embellished with metal or semi-precious stones, or polished to resemble a more valued material such as bronze. Wood was not respected as a material to be used in its natural state until the 20th century.

♦ OAK
Medium-hard, fairly insensitive to changes in humidity and resistant to woodworm, oak was used by medieval sculptors in northern Europe.

♦ LIME
This light-colored wood with the same characteristics as oak has been much used in the Rhine Valley in Germany, where there are huge forests of lime trees.

♦ WALNUT
Walnut, with its warm color and even grain, is popular throughout Europe. It is suitable for smooth sculptures with no decoration.

♦ PEAR
The wood of the pear tree is compact and evenly colored. It is often left without decoration.

♦ PINE
Much used in northern Europe, pine is soft and light, but still resistant to woodworm because of its high resin content.

WORKING METHOD ♦
The artist continues shaping the statue using a series of gouges and chisels.

Chisel.

PREPARATION ♦
Having chosen the most suitable piece of wood, the artist removes the bark and the bumps. For the first stage of rough-shaping the statue he uses an adze and a hatchet.

THE HATCHET ♦
The blade is parallel to the handle. It is used to square the piece of wood.

♦ SEASONING
The wood is left for a long period – a season – at an even temperature in a dry environment. This decreases the humidity contained in its fibers and so prevents expansion and contraction of the finished sculpture.

ROTATING WORK ♦
The sculpture is held firmly, in a horizontal position, between two rotating shafts. This gives the sculptor the convenience of being able to turn the statue round, to work easily on all aspects of it.

◆ TOOLS ◆
The flat-bladed chisel carves the wood in straight planes. The gouge, with its curved cutting edge, is used for hollowing and making grooves.

◆ HISTORY
Wood has always been widely used for sculpture. However, the vast numbers of wooden sculptures produced in ancient times have almost all been lost. Ancient Egyptian sculptures do remain in excellent condition,

◆ GERMAN WOODCARVING
An altar-piece carved by Veit Stoss in the 15th century for Bamberg cathedral.

ANNUNCIATION ◆
Church at San Gimignano, 1421. The painting was not always done by the sculptor. This sculpture by Jacopo della Quercia was painted by Martino di Bartolomeo.

◆ SAWS
Saws are used for rough-shaping. Medieval artists tried to adapt their tools to the different types of wood, and so a wide variety of saws was produced.

because they were preserved in a very hot, dry climate. Tiny cult objects, groups of small statues portraying workmen doing their jobs, and large, rounded statues of pharaohs and dignitaries are all proof of the great talent of the Egyptians and of the popularity of carving wood. A great deal of wooden sculpture was made throughout the Middle Ages, but it enjoyed a period of exceptional splendor in northern European workshops from the 15th to the 17th centuries. Wood was highly valued for the great Baroque statues and is widely used by sculptors today.

THE VILLAGE CHIEF ◆
An ancient Egyptian wooden sculpture from the 4th Dynasty period, 2723-2563 BC (Egyptian Museum, Cairo). The sculptor made the arms separately and then glued them to the bust. The stick the figure is holding is a sign of his aristocratic rank.

◆ RECLINING FIGURE
Wooden sculpture by Henry Moore (Irina Moore Collection, 1959-64).

◆ MALLETS ◆
The cylindrical mallet is best for working on wood.

◆ HOLLOWING OUT
The statue is hollowed out from behind to make it lighter and to prevent the wood from splitting.

SCULPTURE IN TERRACOTTA

Terracotta is clay which is molded and then dried and fired (baked) to make it hard. It was in the later part of the Stone Age that people first used clay, to make domestic objects. Figures and decorations on buildings were also made from terracotta, from very early times. Shaping clay is different from shaping stone and wood, for clay can be added as well as removed, to achieve the form required. When clay is fired it shrinks by about one-tenth of its volume and is likely to crack. Consequently, in ancient times, before the technique was refined, people produced only small terracotta objects. The Etruscans (8th-2nd centuries BC) made larger objects by producing them in two parts which were fired separately and then stuck together with liquid clay. Terracotta was often decorated with painted designs, and it was glazed to make it waterproof and smooth. In the 15th century a sculptor in Florence, Luca della Robbia, developed the use of colored, glazed terracotta. His sculptures of the Madonna and Child in white on a blue background are particularly famous.

♦ CHRIST AND MARY MAGDALENE
This altar-piece from c.1520 (Museo Nazionale del Bargello, Florence) was sculpted by Giovanni Francesco Rustici and glazed by Giovanni della Robbia, a relative of Luca. The yellow background is unusual.

FIRING ♦
After a first firing, to remove moisture, the object was set aside to become solid and hard. A second firing fixed the colored glaze.

THE DESIGN ♦
The artist made a sketch, then drew the design to the actual size of the intended sculpture. The drawing was divided into sections to match the separate blocks of clay from which the work would be made.

MODELING ♦
The artist modeled the clay first of all with his hands. Suitable tools were used to remove excess material and finish off all the details.

CLAY ♦
Before modeling began, the clay had to be prepared. It was passed through a series of washing tubs, to remove any impurities from it.

♦ THE KILN
The kiln had to be kept at an even temperature, as sudden changes would cause damage to the object being fired.

♦ LAMENTATION
A group mourning the death of Christ, modeled by Guido Mazzoni for San Giovanni Battista, Modena, c. 1480-1500. The characters seem to be drawn from real life of the time and from medieval religious drama.

♦ STATUETTES
These small clay female figures date from the 4th-5th millennia BC (Vorderasiatisches Museum, Berlin).

♦ TIMING
Removing the sculpture from the kiln too soon or too late might spoil it. So it was important to time the firing with great care.

♦ ETRUSCAN VASE
An object of everyday use becomes a splendid portrait, c.500 BC (Museo Archeologico, Tarquinia, Italy).

♦ HISTORY
Examples of terracotta objects from ancient times include pottery, small cult objects, and architectural decoration. Terracotta work flourished in Etruria in the 7th to the 2nd centuries BC. The Etruscans sculpted sarcophagi (tombs) and large religious statues. Terracotta regained popularity in the Renaissance: Donatello, Antonio and Piero Pollaiuolo, the della Robbias, Guido Mazzoni and Niccolò dell'Arca were outstanding sculptors of that time. Between the 17th and the 19th centuries, terracotta was used only for preparatory models. By experimenting with materials, 20th-century sculptors have rediscovered the possibilities of the ancient methods.

♦ PAINTING
After its first firing, each piece of the sculpture was dipped in glaze and painted. After the second firing the glaze became fixed, hard and glossy.

HUSBAND AND WIFE ♦
The Etruscan sculptor of this sarcophagus of about 520-510 BC has shown an everyday scene: a couple reclining, as at a banquet (Louvre, Paris).

♦ COLORS
The paint had to withstand high temperatures without changing color. The four basic colors used were blue – which withstood up to 2500° Fahrenheit – yellow, purple and green.

♦ ASSEMBLY
The master checked that the pieces were correctly assembled before firing.

♦ LIGHT-WEIGHT
An assistant scraped material off the back of the panel so that the completed work would not be too heavy.

♦ WATER
As long as the sculptors were at work, the clay was kept wet, so that it was always malleable and ready for use.

AMERICA BEFORE COLUMBUS

Over a period of about 3,000 years, numerous civilizations developed and then disappeared in Central, South and North America, long before the arrival of Columbus and other Europeans. These civilizations were closed and isolated and, with the exception of the Maya, had no form of writing. They used a picture language, which is difficult to decipher. On the other hand, the works of art of these pre-Columbian cultures – their buildings and their sculpture – do serve to tell us about their customs, social structure and beliefs about the afterlife. Around the 1st millennium BC, artists in Mexico carved colossal stone heads, and in the Andes the Moche created extraordinary ceramics. It is hard to believe that the wheel had not been discovered and only simple stone tools were used.

♦ **TOLTEC FIGURES**
Tula in Mexico was the most important city of the warlike Toltec people, who controlled most of central Mexico between AD 900 and 1150. At the top of the pyramid at Tula stand four gigantic pillar-shaped figures. They look like soldiers and each bears a large butterfly on its chest. In previous American civilizations most art had been religious, but the Toltecs began to represent secular subjects too.

♦ **MESOAMERICA**
The first great culture in Mesoamerica (the area from Mexico to Honduras and El Salvador) was that of the Olmecs, which lasted from 1500 to 100 BC. This was the base from which the later civilizations arose, each with its own characteristics: the Totonacs (6th-10th centuries), the Toltecs (10th-12th centuries), the Aztecs (13th-15th centuries) and the Maya.

OLMEC HEAD ♦
This colossal basalt head, found at La Venta, in Tabasco, Mexico, is 2.5 meters (8.2 feet) high and 6 meters (19.7 feet) around. It dates from 1000 BC. Many such Olmec sculptures, with faces depicting different characteristics, show that the Olmecs had become quite skilled at portraiture. (Parco-Museo di La Venta, Villahermosa, Tabasco).

♦ **A TOTONAC GOD**
This small figure with its smiling face and its arms held high is a typical sculpture of the Totonac civilization (Museo Pigorini, Rome).

♦ **PORTRAIT POTTERY**
Ceramics were one of the most important forms of art in the Moche culture which developed between 300 BC and AD 600 along the northern coast of what is today Peru. A wide variety of subjects were used to decorate pots like those shown here, with their characteristic circular handles. Some of the head-shaped pots have individual features and facial expressions and detailed clothing, which suggest that the Moche were portraying real people.

1. *Male head* (Museo Pigorini, Rome);
2. *Male head* (private collection, Milan);
3. *Women sitting* (Museo Pigorini, Rome);
4. *Owl* (Museo Pigorini, Rome).

♦ **ANDEAN AMERICA**
During the 6th and 7th centuries, the San Augustín and Tierradentro cultures prospered between Mesoamerica and the Central Andes, in what is now Colombia. Gigantic human figures with cat features are typical of this area. In the northern Andes, in what is now Ecuador, the Chorrera culture (1000-300 BC) developed in the north and the Jama-Coaque (7th century BC-2nd century AD) in the south, where small terracotta works provide a rare insight into daily life and religious customs. The Chavín civilization (1000-500 BC) was the main culture of the central Andes, now Peru. It developed between the Andes and the Amazon, and spread the worship of deities like the Cayman-god and the Sceptre-god throughout that area. Later cultures also portrayed these gods.

1

3

4

♦ **A MAZE OF BAS-RELIEFS**
Chanchán was the political and religious center of the powerful Chimú kingdom, established between the 12th and the 14th centuries along the northern coast of what is today Peru. The monumental center of the city, built from huge clay blocks, is made up of ten enclosures each containing dwellings, public buildings, roads and a necropolis (burial site). The walls of the buildings are patterned with molded animal and geometric designs, making a stunning overall effect.

♦ **NORTHERN ANDES**
A sandstone sculpture found in the northern Andes (Ecuador) (Museo Pigorini, Rome).

THE RENAISSANCE

A great movement of artistic and cultural rebirth ("renaissance" in French) developed in Florence and other Italian cities during the early 15th century. Artists, architects and sculptors looked back for inspiration to ancient Greek and Roman styles and ideas. In their own cities, they could study examples of classical Roman sculpture: statues and low-reliefs on columns, triumphal arches and sarcophagi. And so it was in sculpture, ahead of painting and architecture, that the new interest in classical styles was first expressed. Some examples are Bernardo Rossellino's tomb of Leonardo Bruni, the chancellor of the Florentine Republic, which draws on a range of classical sources; Nanni di Banco's *Four Saints*, figures which resemble Roman sculptures of severe-looking senators; and Donatello's *putti* (cupids), which look like characters from scenes on some Roman sarcophagi.

♦ MONUMENT TO A HUMANIST
Bernardo Rossellino (1409-64) trained with Leon Battista Alberti, a famous architect and art theorist. Rossellino blended architecture and sculpture in the tomb he carved for the humanist Leonardo Bruni, in the church of Santa Croce in Florence, 1444-50. It became the model for the large number of tombs that Florentine sculptors worked on during the rest of the 15th century. Humanist ideas, which arose with the Renaissance, encouraged the practice of honoring the memory of outstanding men.

Frieze from the tomb of Helena, Rome, AD c.320 (Musei Vaticani, Rome).

Nobleman, late 4th century BC (Museo Archeologico, Tarquinia, Italy).

LIKE AN ETRUSCAN ♦
Showing the dead person lying on the sarcophagus was an Etruscan custom.

THE EAGLE ♦
The eagle was a symbol of power, used by Roman legions on their standards.

From the base of Trajan's column, Rome, 2nd century AD.

PUTTI ♦
The frieze with *putti* holding up festoons matches sculptures on tombs of 1400 years earlier.

♦ ANGELS
The angels holding up the laurel wreath resemble figures found on a Roman sarcophagus.

From a tomb,
late 1st century AD
(British Museum,
London).

♦ **THE VIRGIN MARY**
The circular relief
portrait derives
directly from Roman
portraiture.

♦ **LEAVES**
The laurel-leaf- and
palm-leaf-like
decorations on the
arch were inspired by
details seen on
classical monuments.

Corinthian capital.

♦ **CLASSICAL DESIGN**
The two pilasters
framing the niche
and supporting the
arch are topped with
Corinthian capitals.
The architectural
design of the tomb
blends with the
sculpture.

From the base of Trajan's column.

♦ **SEEN IN ROME**
The winged figures
holding the plaque
are almost identical
to those on the base
of Trajan's column.

♦ **FEROCIOUS BEASTS**
The small lion's head
in the center of the
frieze was an echo of
a motif used fairly
frequently in ancient
sculpture.

Lion's head,
3rd century BC
(Palazzo dei
Conservatori, Rome).

♦ **DONATELLO**
Donatello (1386-
1466) was one of the
creators of the
Renaissance style in
Florence. His bronze
David (left) of c.1433
(Museo Nazionale
del Bargello,
Florence) was the
first free-standing,
life-size nude statue
since the classical
age. Above, the
*Portrait of Niccolò da
Uzzano* (Museo
Nazionale del
Bargello), an
opponent of the
Medici family, looks
like a bust from
Republican Rome.

♦ **NANNI DI BANCO**
Nanni di Banco (1380s-
1421) was another of
the creators of the
Renaissance in
Florence. In the lower
panel of the *Tabernacle
for the Guild of
Stonemasons* (Or
San Michele,
Florence), 1414, his
carvings of
stonemasons and
sculptors resemble
ancient Roman
sculpture.

♦ **JACOPO DELLA
QUERCIA**
A sculptor from
Siena, della Quercia
(1371-1438) brought
both Gothic elegance
and drama into his
classical-style works.
Rea Silvia (below) of
1414-19 (Palazzo
Pubblico, Siena) is
based on a Roman
model: Venus the
mother holding her
children close.

**GHIBERTI ♦
AND BRUNELLESCHI**
Ghiberti (1378-1455)
and Brunelleschi
(1377-1446) entered a
competition in 1401,
for the job of
sculpting new bronze
doors for the
baptistery of Florence
Cathedral. They
submitted sample
panels of *The
Sacrifice of Isaac*. In
his winning panel
(top) Ghiberti's
figure of Isaac looks
like a Greek nude
figure. In the bottom
right of
Brunelleschi's panel
(below) a servant is
modeled on a Roman
figure of a boy
removing a thorn
from his foot.

MICHELANGELO AND MARBLE

One of the greatest artists of the Renaissance, Michelangelo said that it is the stone itself that inspires the sculptor – for it is as if the sculpture already exists, imprisoned in it. The sculptor's job is to release the statue from the block by removing the excess stone. The stone Michelangelo used was marble, quarried in the Apuan Alps in Tuscany. He often visited the quarries to choose his own material. He paid great attention to the quality of the marble and gave the quarry workers detailed instructions about the shape he needed, and the way to cut the block. Sometimes he even described the size of every part of the new sculpture he had in mind. Michelangelo involved himself intensely in all stages of his work, from choosing the marble to carving the final detail. Unlike other artists, he did not delegate any stage, and this led to his being unable to finish all the works he started.

♦ THE APUAN ALPS
In Tuscany, very near the Tyrrhenian Sea, these mountains take their name from the ancient inhabitants of the region. The mountain tops look white, as if they are under snow. But what looks like snow is, in fact, marble.

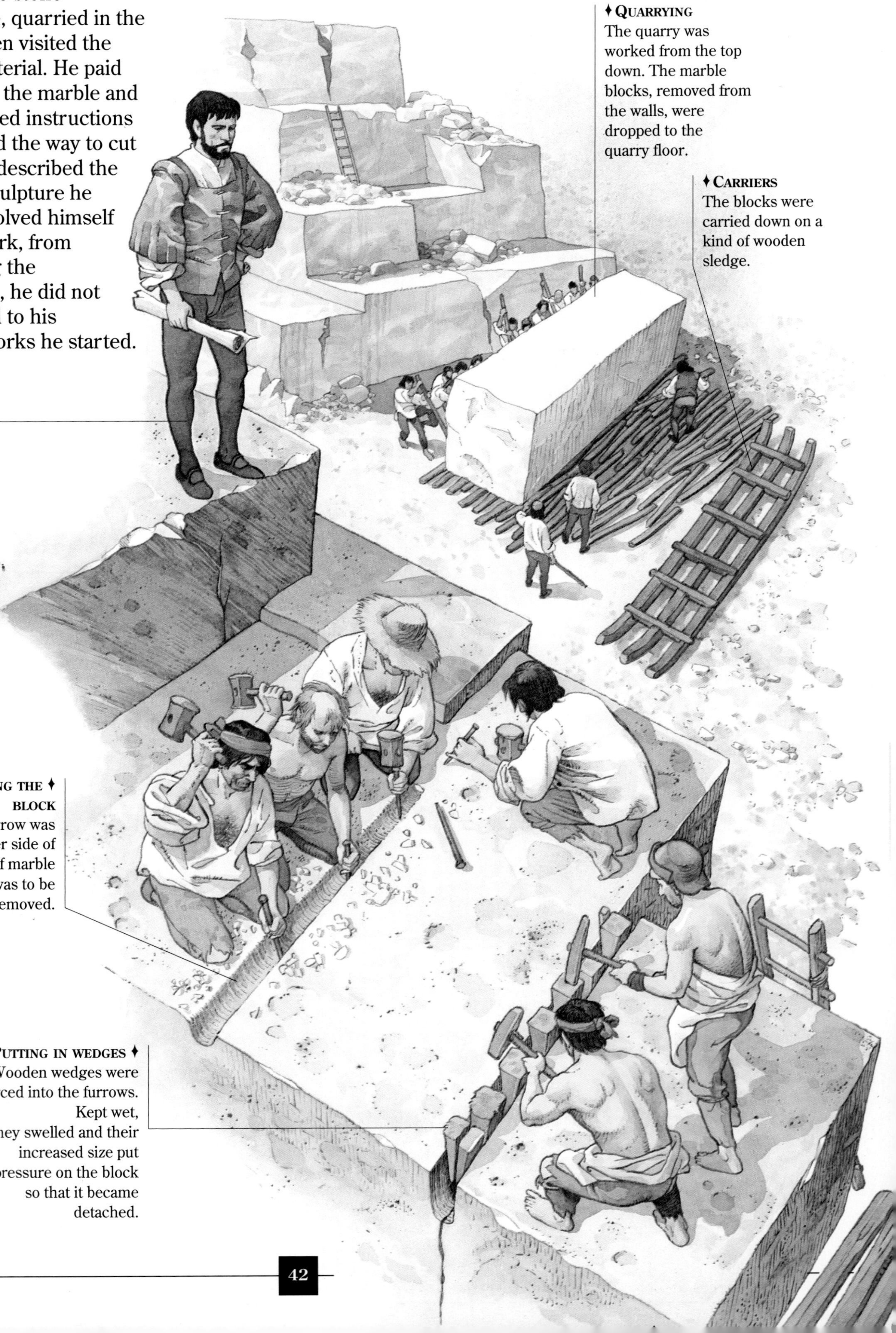

♦ QUARRYING
The quarry was worked from the top down. The marble blocks, removed from the walls, were dropped to the quarry floor.

♦ CARRIERS
The blocks were carried down on a kind of wooden sledge.

MICHELANGELO ♦
He watched the quarrymen closely. The stone chosen would have a great influence on the finished work and so he liked to know everything he could about it.

SEPARATING THE ♦ BLOCK
A deep furrow was dug on either side of the block of marble that was to be removed.

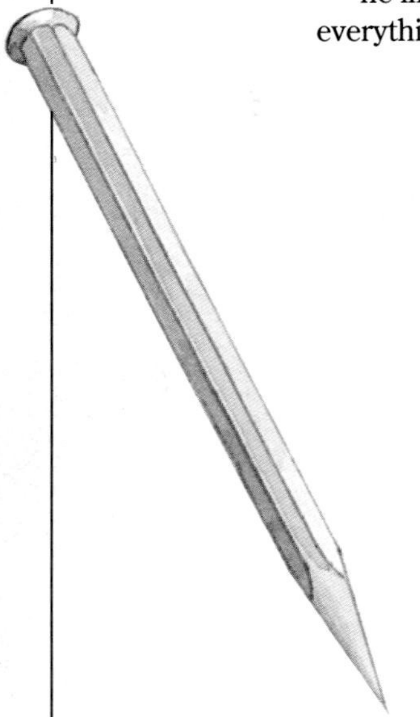

♦ CHISEL
The quarry workers would cut into the stone using a long iron chisel head like the one shown above, which they struck with a mallet. This was one of the most used tools in the quarry.

PUTTING IN WEDGES ♦
Wooden wedges were forced into the furrows. Kept wet, they swelled and their increased size put pressure on the block so that it became detached.

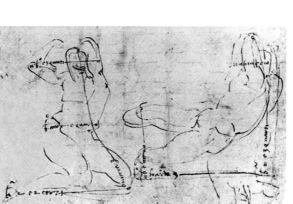

♦ MARBLES IN THE APUAN ALPS
Exploitation of the Apuan Alps began in the 1st century BC and continued until the 4th-5th centuries AD. Then the high cost of extracting marble and the wide availability of salvage material caused the quarries to close. Large-scale operations began again in the 15th century when the Opera del Duomo (Cathedral Vestry Board) in Florence took its supply from the mountains. Michelangelo favored white Carrara marble, and this very smooth type was used almost exclusively in the Neoclassical period (17th-19th centuries). Marbles from the Apuan Alps are still considered some of the best today.

LOWERING THE ♦ BLOCKS
The blocks of marble were lowered on the "sledges", controlled by ropes.

♦ THE ROPES
The speed with which the load was lowered was controlled by slackening and holding the ropes.

DESIGN ♦
A sketch by Michelangelo for the stone cutters, 1525 (British Museum, London).

POSTS ♦
To make the ropes easier to handle, they were wound around wooden or marble posts fixed into the ground by the side of the track.

LEVERING ♦
The load was also moved by levering it with poles.

THE SUPERVISOR ♦
An expert was needed who was able to co-ordinate the various parts of the operation of lowering the stone.

♦ PRECAUTIONS
To save the blocks of marble from breaking when they dropped, a bed of tree trunks was made for them to fall on to.

ROLLERS ♦
The sledge slid along on pieces of wood lubricated with soap and placed along the track. As the load moved forwards, the rollers were collected from behind and placed in front.

THE MARBLE GOVERNS THE SHAPE

Imagine a figure completely immersed in a tub of water. If the plug is removed the tub will start to empty and the figure will begin to emerge from the water. When the first parts protrude above the surface of the water, the figure will look like a low-relief. When all the water has drained away, then we will see the completely rounded figure. The figure emerging from water is an image of Michelangelo's method of carving. He would begin work on the front of the marble block, to "release" the figure contained within it. Like Greek sculptors, he drew the figure on the face of the stone. However, he did not work all around the statue. He carved deeper and deeper, always from the front, and the figures gradually emerged from the material. Michelangelo's unfinished works may look as if they were intended to be low-reliefs, but this is not the case. They are completely rounded figures which he had still to uncover.

♦ MICHELANGELO
Michelangelo Buonarotti (1475-1564) was famous in his twenties for his sculptures of *Bacchus* and *David* in Florence and the *Pietà* in St Peter's, Rome. He competed with Leonardo da Vinci to paint a mural in the Council Chamber of the Palazzo Vecchio (Florence). At thirty-three, he was commissioned by Pope Julius II to paint the ceiling of the Sistine Chapel in the Vatican, 1508-12. Michelangelo also designed the Medici Chapel and the Biblioteca Laurenziana at San Lorenzo church, Florence. His painting of the *Last Judgement* on the rear wall of the Sistine Chapel, unveiled in 1541, was darker than his earlier work. Two more sculptures of the *Pietà*, unfinished when he died, were also different in mood from the first one.

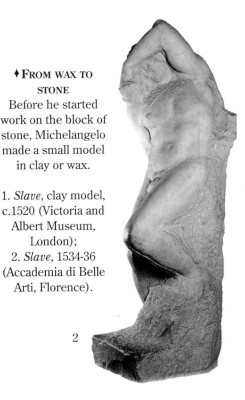

♦ FROM WAX TO STONE
Before he started work on the block of stone, Michelangelo made a small model in clay or wax.

1. *Slave*, clay model, c.1520 (Victoria and Albert Museum, London);
2. *Slave*, 1534-36 (Accademia di Belle Arti, Florence).

1   2

THE GOUGE ♦
Michelangelo used the gouge for the first stage of work: rough-shaping the hard surface of the stone.

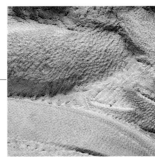

THE CHISEL ♦
He used the end of the chisel to outline on the marble the basic shapes of the various parts of the sculpture. The chisel lines were still visible when the work was completed.

♦ UNFINISHED
Michelangelo left a large number of sculptures which he had not been able to finish, such as this *Atlas* (Accademia di Belle Arti, Florence), 1534-36. The unfinished sculptures show us the stages in which he worked, and the various tools he used.

♦ SLOW WORK
A figure emerged slowly from the material. As he worked deeper, Michelangelo completed the protruding parts while those further back were still at the rough-shaped stage.

✦ RELEASING THE SHAPE

Dying slave, c.1513 (Louvre, Paris). Every part of this figure has been completely finished. Only the mass at the base remains as a reminder of the shapeless stone block in which the figure was hidden and from which it has been released.

✦ PIETÀ

A *Pietà* is an image of the Virgin Mary with the dead Christ across her knees. This sculpture of 1497-98 (St Peter's, Rome) is one of Michelangelo's most finished works. The surface of the stone is perfectly smooth, with no trace of the tools used.

✦ THE RONDANINI PIETÀ

Towards the end of his life, after 1552, Michelangelo returned to work on a *Pietà* that he had begun in earlier days (Castello Sforza, Milan). He kept some of the finished areas, such as the legs and the right arm of the Christ figure, but he began to reduce the size of the rest of the sculpture. He returned some of it to the rough-shaping stage. The effect of his reworking is to make the sculpture look highly expressive.

✦ THE CLAW CHISEL

The claw chisel allows the sculptor to make parallel lines on the marble, so that it looks as if it has been raked. It is used to engrave the surface and to dig deeply into the stone.

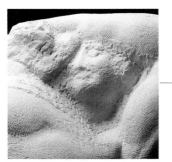

✦ HATCHING

Michelangelo used the claw chisel to make criss-cross lines on the marble, similar to shading in sketches. This gave a sense of light and shade, enhancing the sculpture's contours.

✦ USING A DRILL

This tool is used to perforate the marble, to achieve otherwise unobtainable results. Michelangelo rarely used a drill, but he clearly did so to create the pupils and the curls of *David*.

✦ POLISHING

Michelangelo rubbed his works with abrasive powder or stone like pumice, to remove flaws from the surface. Completely finished works were given a high polish.

✦ TRANSPORT

The stone blocks were transported by sea, but there was also a great deal of ground to cover from the quarry to the port. Once the blocks of marble had been lowered to the valley floor, they were loaded onto large wooden carts. These were drawn by many pairs of oxen. Great numbers of men accompanied the load along roads that were often blocked by stones and extremely muddy in winter. A man sat on the yoke of each pair of oxen to drive the animals.

POINTS OF VIEW

Until the middle of the 16th century sculptors thought of their statues as having a "front" – the main side to be viewed – even though they modeled them all round. But later, ideas changed and statues were created to be viewed from many angles. To appreciate a statue fully, the viewer now had to walk around it. One reason for this change was the sculptors' new attitude to their work, which reflected general ideas of the time as expressed, for example, by Baldassare Castiglione. Hard, physical work was considered degrading for a creative artist, and so the sculptor would design a statue by making small wax or clay models and leave the hard labor of carving the stone to his workshop assistants. As he worked out the design, the sculptor would turn the models over in his hands, studying them from all angles, and so the finished statue was made to be viewed in a similar way. The separation of the sculpting work from the designing gave late 16th-century sculptors an attitude to their work that was entirely different from Michelangelo's. For him, the shape of the stone inspired the shape of the statue. For them, the shape of the stone had no such meaning. Several blocks of stone were needed for many of their statues.

♦ **NO EFFORT**
In 1528 Baldassarre Castiglione's book, *The Courtier*, was published throughout Europe. It put forward the idea that the perfect gentleman was well-educated and self-confident and did everything effortlessly. Hard work was not for gentlemen or artists. Right: *Castiglione* by Raphael, c.1515 (Louvre, Paris).

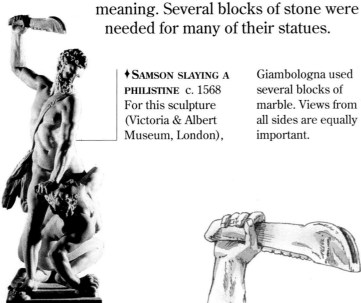

♦ **SAMSON SLAYING A PHILISTINE** c. 1568 For this sculpture (Victoria & Albert Museum, London), Giambologna used several blocks of marble. Views from all sides are equally important.

♦ **COBBLED TOGETHER**
Michelangelo was scornful of sculptors who used several blocks of stone to make one statue, and Giorgio Vasari (1511-74), a painter and architect who wrote about the Italian Renaissance artists in his famous book *The Lives of the Artists*, described such statues as "cobbled together". However, artists found increasing need to use several blocks of stone for one work, and by the following, Baroque period, this had become the convention.

♦ MANNERISM

"Mannerism" is the term used to describe Italian art between the Renaissance and the Baroque. At this time artists tried to surpass the works of the Renaissance by displays of virtuosity that were often exaggerated. Two works by Cellini while he was at Fontainebleau are (left) a bronze relief of the *Nymph of Fontainebleau* (Louvre, Paris), 1542-45, and (right) a gold *salt-cellar* made for Francis I, 1540-43 (Kunsthistorisches Museum, Vienna). The elongated limbs are typical of the Fontainebleau school.

♦ FONTAINEBLEAU

Francis I, King of France (1494–1547), called many artists, mostly from Italy, to decorate his palace at Fontainebleau. Rosso and Primaticcio were the most well-known. They adapted their style to match French tastes, and the Mannerist style soon spread throughout Europe. Right: detail of stucco work by Primaticcio.

♦ PERSEUS

Benvenuto Cellini (1500-71) cast this bronze figure of *Perseus*, for the Loggia dei Lanzi, Florence, in 1553. There were problems with the casting as the bronze contained too much copper and would not melt. Cellini solved the problem by adding some of his household utensils made of tin and lead. Cellini was a goldsmith and sculptor, who worked first in Rome, then from 1540-45 at Fontainebleau, and after that mainly in Florence, for Cosimo I de' Medici. His racy autobiography pictures the life of a Renaissance craftsman.

♦ THE RAPE OF A SABINE

This statue by Giambologna, 1581-82, is situated in the center of the Loggia dei Lanzi in Florence. This covered open space is an ideal place for a statue intended to be viewed from every angle. Giambologna set himself the challenge of incorporating three figures into the group and of making a sculpture which was to be viewed by walking all around it, and not just by looking at it from a certain number of set points. The statue shows the abduction of a Sabine woman by a Roman. Beneath the legs of the Roman, an older man watches the scene with horror. The three figures in relation to each other make a spiral shape. Several small wax models survive, and one can imagine how Giambologna would have turned these in his hands and studied them, to work out how to achieve the final effect he wanted.

♦ MERCURY

Flemish-born Giambologna (1529-1608), also known as Jean Boulogne, sculpted the Fountain of Neptune for Bologna, but worked mainly in Florence where he made this Mercury (Museo Nazionale del Bargello, Florence), 1564-65. He also made bronze statuettes, which were popular. Being portable, they played a part in making the Mannerist style known throughout Europe.

THE BAROQUE

The Baroque style of art began in Italy and flourished in Europe in the 17th century. By this time, the theory of the scientist Copernicus, that the earth was not the center of the universe, but revolved around the sun, had begun to take hold. It can be argued that this idea led artists to take a new interest in showing the natural world as in a constant state of change. An important feature of a Baroque work of art is that all parts of it are in harmony and balance. Painting, sculpture and architecture are used together, to create a single grand effect. A well-known example of such a combination of the three arts is the Palace of Versailles. The aim of the Baroque artist is to create an illusion of a real setting, in which the observer feels involved. This illusion of reality is achieved by the use of colors and strong contrasts of light and dark. Gianlorenzo Bernini was the greatest of the Baroque sculptors. His statue of *Apollo and Daphne* is an example of a sculpture depicting nature as constantly changing. His Chair of St Peter, in St Peter's, Rome, is an example of Baroque illusionistic art.

✦ ILLUSIONS
Baroque sculptors worked together to design and build fantastic machines which were paraded at festivals and on solemn occasions. Catafalques (tomb-like structures) crammed with statues, complicated self-propelled inventions, and huge wood and papier-mâché models were quickly created and then destroyed immediately after use. For the Spanish Infanta, who came to Rome in 1651, Bernini made an extraordinary elephant, 8 meters (26 feet) high, which breathed fire and flames from its trunk.

A LEAFY BRANCH ✦
Daphne's hair has turned into a leafy branch.

LEAVES ✦
The fingers have already changed into leaves.

✦ APOLLO AND DAPHNE
This work by Bernini (Galleria Borghese, Rome), from the period 1622-25, was one of a series of life-size marble statues created for Cardinal Scipione Borghese. It represents a classical Greek myth, as told by the Latin poet Ovid in his *Metamorphoses*.

✦ TRANSFORMATION
The delicately worked marble seems to change consistency, from soft skin to hard bark and new, unfurling leaves. This reflects the constant transformations that occur in nature.

✦ BARK
The legs and hips become encased within the bark.

ROOTS ✦
Fine roots sprout from Daphne's toes and run into the ground.

✦ THE MYTH
An ancient Greek myth tells how Apollo became infatuated with Daphne, daughter of the river god Peneus, and tried to make love to her. She ran from him and he followed. As he caught up, near the river, Daphne called to her father, asking him to change her form to help her escape from Apollo. At the water's edge, her feet became rooted to the ground and she was changed into a laurel tree.

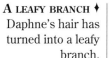

♦CHAIR OF ST PETER
Pope Alexander VII commissioned Bernini to sculpture the *Chair of St Peter* at St Peter's, Rome, 1656-66, in the apse of the church. With angels on either side, overhung by clouds and cherubs and supported by four magnificent bronzes of the Fathers of the Church, the throne seems to reach up into heaven.

LIGHT ♦
A golden light shines from the oval window where the dove of the Holy Spirit is depicted. This represented the light of God which fell on the Church and blessed its popes.

RELIEFS ♦
The low-reliefs of clouds and little angels in the background combine with the large, fully rounded figures of the Church Fathers, to create a living scene which looks like a miraculous event in the church.

♦COLORS
The bronze contrasts with the colored marble and the glowing, gilded plaster of the upper section. The colors were not meant to imitate nature but to produce the supernatural effect of a religious vision.

THE ECSTASY OF ♦
ST THERESA
Painting, sculpture and architecture are skilfully combined in this marble group which Bernini made in 1647-51 for the Cornaro Chapel in Santa Maria della Vittoria, Rome.

♦SPACE
The proportions of the various parts of the sculpture, the colors, the use of perspective and the lighting all create an illusion of space. The whole construction appears like a great theatrical backdrop.

♦THE FIGURES
Saints Augustine, Ambrose, Anastasius and John Chrysostom hold onto St Peter's throne. By supporting the papal seat, the four Church Fathers underline the authority of the Church of Rome.

♦WATER
Bernini's *Fountain of the Four Rivers*, which he sculpted for Pope Innocent X in the Piazza Navona, Rome, 1648-51. Running water was a favorite element of Baroque sculpture.

♦GIANLORENZO BERNINI
(1598-1680) Born in Naples, the son of a sculptor, Bernini applied himself to this art from an early age, studying 16th-century masters and ancient works. Cardinal Scipione Borghese commissioned him to sculpt *Aeneas, Anchises and Ascanius*, *The Rape of Proserpine*, *David* and *Apollo and Daphne*, 1619-25, and throughout his life he received commissions from nobles and popes. He created the *Baldacchino* (canopy over the altar) in St Peter's, Rome, 1624-33, sculpted the *Chair*, and designed the colonnade around the piazza in front of the church, 1656-67. He graced Rome with fountains, buildings and the *Equestrian Statue of Constantine* for the Scala Regia, 1657-66. His many portait busts include one of *Louis XIV*, 1665, above (Louvre, Paris).

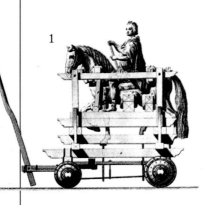
1

THE ENLIGHTENMENT

In the 18th century, which is sometimes described as the Age of Enlightenment, philosophers believed in the power of human reason to answer all problems. The art of the time reflects that philosophy. Edmé Bouchardon's *Equestrian Statue of Louis XV*, sculpted between 1748 and 1763, is an example of how methodical 18th-century artists were. Bouchardon studied other famous equestrian monuments: the ancient statue of Marcus Aurelius, Bernini's statue of *Constantine*, the one of *Henry IV* by Giambologna and Pietro Tacca, and Girardon's statue of *Louis XIV*. He then made four hundred preparatory drawings, followed by a series of wax and terracotta models. It took him four years to make the plaster model, and another two to organize the lost-wax casting, for which a special building had to be put up. Many important people attended the casting, which took place on Saturday, 6 May 1758, at 4:20 p.m., and lasted five minutes and four seconds. The result was perfect. A book commemorating the operation is the only record left, as the statue was destroyed in 1792 during the French Revolution.

♦**THE MONUMENT**
Edmé Bouchardon (Chaumont, 1698-Paris, 1762) spent fourteen years sculpting the *Equestrian Statue of Louis XV*, erected in Paris in the square now called the Place de la Concorde. It was 5.2 meters (17 feet) high, the largest bronze cast ever made. Bouchardon proved himself an able contractor, co-ordinating the work of many engineers, metalworkers, bricklayers, plaster-workers and blacksmiths.

2

3

♦**STUDIES**
In his preparatory drawings, Bouchardon studied details of the horse and rider from every angle.

1. and 5. From the book about the casting by Jean-Pierre Mariette, Paris, 1786; 2., 3. and 4. Cabinet des Dessins, Paris.

4

INSIDE ♦
The interior of the model was supported by a complex iron framework. It could not all be removed before casting and some pieces remained inside the finished statue.

5

THE CAST ♦
Built inside a great pit, the cast was made of fire-resistant bricks, and held together with strong, iron brackets.

THE PIT ♦
The pit was lined with a thick stone wall, which enclosed the whole structure built for the casting.

BUTTRESSES ♦
A bricklayer completes work on one of the brick buttresses that supported the cast.

HOLES
Casting holes and air vents were left in the top of the cast.

THE FURNACE
The molten bronze poured through the pipe from the furnace.

SMOKE
Holes were left in the layer of bricks covering the pit, so that the smoke could escape.

FILLING
Before casting began, the pit was packed with waste bricks to prevent excessive heat loss.

DUCTS
The melted wax was discharged from the cast through several ducts like this one.

PASSAGEWAY
An underground passageway gave access to the casting pit.

WAX
At each corner of the pit, there was a shaft filled with water, into which the melted wax was discharged.

HEATING
Putting wood to be burned in the tunnel around the cast. The heat melted the wax.

CANOVA: FROM PLASTER TO MARBLE

Antonio Canova was one of the most esteemed sculptors of the Neoclassical movement in the late 18th and early 19th centuries. Neoclassical artists were interested again in creating work in the style of classical Greece and Rome. To make his smooth, weightless-looking marble statues, Canova worked in several stages. First he sketched on paper his ideas for the composition of the sculpture. Then the sketches were turned into small models. These models of the figure in different positions were extremely realistic, conveying feeling and movement and physical effort. Next a plaster model was made, of the actual size of the final intended sculpture. At this stage, shapes were simplified and the composition became more balanced. Finally, the plaster model was copied in marble. To give the marble statue a pearly glow, it was polished with finer and finer pumice-stones and treated with lightly colored wax in order to reduce the whiteness.

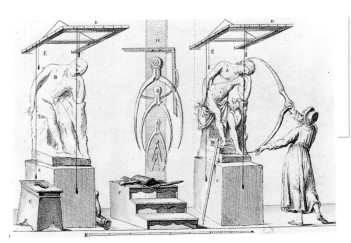

♦AN EARLY FORM OF PANTOGRAPH
This 19th-century drawing illustrates the tools which the sculptor used for making an exact copy of a plaster model in marble, and also for making a larger replica from a small model: a frame, plumb lines, and a series of compasses.

FINISHING TOUCHES ♦
When his studio assistants had almost finished work on a sculpture, Canova stepped in to attend to the final small details.

MODELS ♦
Canova was very possessive of his sketches and models, considering them as personal notes. He kept them in cupboards in his studio.

♦SELF-PORTRAIT
Antonio Canova, 1812 (Plaster Casts Gallery, Possagno).

♦ANTONIO CANOVA
Canova was born in 1757, at Possagno, near Treviso. In 1768 he moved to Venice, where he learned about ancient sculpture from copies and made several nude studies. From 1781 he was in Rome, where he could study classical art first hand. He was soon successful, receiving official commissions for tombs for Popes Clement XIII and Clement XIV and for the *Monument to Maria Christina of Austria*. He ran a large studio, carrying out work for the Duke of Wellington, Napoleon, Catherine the Great of Russia and George IV of England. He died in Venice in 1822.

COMPASS ♦
An assistant, using a suitable compass, checks that the proportions of the plaster model accurately match those of the little clay models made by the master.

♦TOMB OF POPE CLEMENT XIV
The tomb, in Santi Apostoli, Rome, was created by Canova between 1784 and 1787. The two statues on the tomb symbolize Mildness, on the right, and Temperance, on the left.

♦ PAULINE BORGHESE
The plaster model (far left) for this portrait of Napoleon's sister (left, Galleria Borghese, Rome), made between 1804 and 1806, is kept in the Plaster Casts Gallery at Possagno. The nails used as reference points are visible on the model.

LIGHT ♦
Lighting was important in a sculptor's studio. Large windows with shutters allowed the sculptor to check the effect of different lights on his work.

PLUMB LINES ♦
Two identical frames were hung above the plaster model and the block of marble to be sculptured. Plumb lines hanging from the frames made a grid of co-ordinates so that the accuracy of the copy could be checked.

NAILS ♦
Small, copper nails were hammered into the finished plaster statue and used as reference points when making the marble copy.

♦ VISITORS
Canova's studio was a meeting-place for high society. Among the many visitors were some of the famous people who commissioned work from him.

KNIFE-GRINDER ♦
Tools had to be kept sharp at all times.

THE 19TH CENTURY

Until the 19th century artists received their commissions from the Church or from the aristocracy, who therefore controlled the whole art world. Now this began to change. Artists started to work for public institutions and also received commissions from wealthy middle-class people. Even more than painters, sculptors needed to have buyers for their work before they could begin. Materials and the tools required for a sculpture were expensive, and the sculptor would probably need to hire other workers too. Artists found their customers by taking part in exhibitions and through art dealers. A growing interest in contemporary subjects made portraits and public monuments popular. Portraits were easy to house in middle-class homes. Portraits ranging in style from Neoclassical busts to caricatures of contemporary figures, realistic representations of workers and the dramatic works of Rodin are among the wealth of sculpture produced in the 19th century.

✦ JEAN-AUGUSTE BARRE
Barre's bust of the *Empress Eugénie* (Musée National du Château, Compiègne) 1861. The bust was the most commonly used medium for official portraits, inspired by Roman examples.

✦ CITIES OF THE DEAD
The construction of new and larger cemeteries outside city walls made it possible for people to have family tombs, where they could arrange for themselves and their loved ones to be remembered permanently. The tombs were filled with monuments and statues and cemeteries became like cities themselves, housing images of the dead.
Above: François Milhomme, *Sorrow*, c.1816, Père-Lachaise Cemetery, Paris.

✦ A MODERN-DAY COLOSSUS
The *Statue of Liberty Enlightening the World*, which stands at the entrance to New York harbor, was designed by the French sculptor Frédéric-Auguste Bartholdi. Gustave Eiffel designed the framework for it. The entire structure was made in Paris, then packed into 214 crates and sent to New York in 1885. There, it was reassembled. The large copper plates were soldered one by one onto the framework of posts and iron girders. The statue was inaugurated in the Bay of New York on 26 October 1886.

(Top to bottom: Musée National des techniques, Paris; New York Public Library, New York; New York Public Library, New York.)

✦ FRANÇOIS RUDE
François Rude (1784-1855) was a great admirer of Napoleon Bonaparte. He created this monument, entitled *The Awakening of Bonaparte*, for the Parc Noisot in Fixin, near Dijon, in 1845-47. It shows the emperor throwing off his shroud.

✦ CARL ELSHOECHT
Father and Son, 1846 (Musée des Beaux-Arts, Dunkirk). Middle-class customers wanted small portraits conveying a peaceful, harmonious atmosphere.

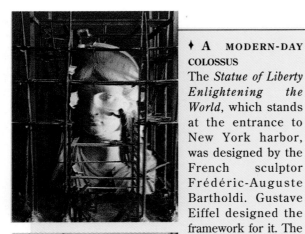

AIMÉ-JULES DALOU ✦
Peasant, 1898-1902. (Musée d'Orsay, Paris). From the 1830s onwards, writers and artists turned to the lives of working people for their subjects, and some sculptors followed suit. This was a time of social reform, to improve conditions for ordinary working people, and some of the sculptors' work added to the protests calling for reform. The first realist sculptures portrayed suffering, hard-working people in a heroic light.

HONORÉ DAUMIER ✦
Caricature became a political weapon. 1. *Charles Philippon*; 2. *Guizot* (Musée d'Orsay, Paris), 1833.

1   2

✦ DAVID D'ANGERS
This bust of the French writer and politician *Chateaubriand* (Musée des Beaux-Arts, Angers) was sculpted by David d'Angers in 1830. Chateaubriand was a leader of the Romantic movement in literature.

✦ CAMILLE CLAUDEL
The sculptress of this bust of *Rodin* (Musée Rodin, Paris), 1888, was his student and companion.

AUGUSTE RODIN ✦
Rodin's sculpture of the author *Balzac* in Boulevard Raspail, Paris, finished in 1898, was thought too radical by the people who had commissioned it. It was not cast and set up until 1939.

✦ THE IMPORTANCE OF RODIN'S WORK
Auguste Rodin (1840-1917) moved sculpture forward in the 19th century, as the Impressionists revolutionized painting. He trained at art schools in Paris, but it was seeing the work of Michelangelo that inspired his sculpture *The Age of Bronze*, in 1876. *Pain*, *The Kiss* and *The Thinker* are some of his most well-known works. Between 1884 and 1886, he created *The Burghers of Calais*. The creativity and sense of movement in his work set a new style for the 20th century.
Left: *The Kiss*, 1901-04 (Musée Rodin, Paris).

OCEANIA

The symbolism and style of art found in the island groups of the Pacific would seem to have come from one single culture because of their striking similarities, even though some islands are many thousands of miles apart. Artists decorated objects intended for everyday use in a symbolic way, which gave the objects magical as well as practical value. For example, door-jambs were made to look like menacing masks, in order to keep evil spirits away from the home; canoes had an image of a god attached to their bow, to protect the people who journeyed in them; a large ivory fishing hook was carved with the image of an ancestor, who would bring good luck to the fisherman. Except for on Easter Island, stone was not much used. Wood was the most widely used material throughout Oceania. However, sculptors also worked with particular local materials such as sea ivory, shells, clay and carefully worked tree-bark.

✦ SHARK
This wooden sculpture with inlaid decoration comes from the Solomon Islands (British Museum, London).

✦ MELANESIA
New Guinea is the region of Oceania most abounding in works of art. Stylized figures painted in unrealistic colors interpret nature without making any attempt to imitate it. Artists often included spiral patterns and animals such as birds, fish and crocodiles in their work. Sculptures with human characteristics, painted black and encrusted with mother-of-pearl, were used to decorate canoes.

✦ MASK
From New Guinea (Musei Vaticani, Rome).

✦ FOR THE BOW OF A DUG-OUT CANOE
To keep evil at bay, this wood figure of a guardian-god would have been mounted on the bow of a boat going to war (Museo Pigorini, Rome).

CREATOR GOD ✦
This large wooden figure, from Rurutu in the Iles Australes, French Polynesia, represents the god Tangaroa, father of all gods, giving life to humans and to the minor gods. The sculpture portrays the act of creation in a fascinating way (British Museum, London).

✦ POLYNESIA

The eastern part of Oceania is known as Polynesia. This area makes a perfect triangle, with New Zealand, Easter Island and the Hawaiian Islands as its three points. Polynesian art was clearly ornamental, with the frequent appearance of geometric patterns. The best-known centers of art in Polynesia were the Marquesas Islands, where the tattoo was developed into an art form, Easter Island with its unusual, stone giants, and New Zealand, inhabited by the Maoris who completely covered their fine wooden sculptures with deeply carved geometric designs. An example of this is shown below.

✦ SEVEN MOAI

These gigantic stone figures on Easter Island, with their elongated heads and roughly shaped bodies, reach a height of 10-12 meters (32-40 feet). They are carved from blocks of volcanic tufa, and stand on purpose-built stone platforms. These extraordinary figures are thought to represent local ancestors, but it is a mystery why they were sculpted on a bleak hillside, all with their backs to the sea.

HUMAN FACE ✦

Maori art of New Zealand. This wood sculpture with eyes made from mother-of-pearl would have been used to decorate a home (Museo Pigorini, Rome).

GUARDIAN-GOD ✦

This god would be placed at the entrance to a dwelling to keep away evil spirits. (Museo di Antropologia e Etnologia, Florence).

MAORI ART ✦

The New Zealand Maoris, who were skilled wood sculptors, specialized in elaborate carving (Museum of Primitive Art, New York).

AFRICAN SCULPTURE

Sculpture was the main form of art used by the different tribal societies in Africa. The aim of tribal art was not to capture a picture of the world as it really is, or to make an ideal image of it. The purpose of this art was rarely decorative. Rather, tribal art was linked with the supernatural and magic. Small sculptures symbolizing strength and courage were offered to a warrior so that he would feel stronger and braver in battle. The witch doctor had a mask whose painted eyes had a powerful stare to strike fear and respect into those he would heal. A figure of a woman with children was used to ensure fertility, and a simplified face rather than a detailed portrait was carved to evoke the invisible kingdom of the dead. In the 20th century, the non-realistic, more abstract nature of African art has excited and given new inspiration to Western artists.

1

2

3

4

♦ ANCESTORS

African tribal people believed that their dead ancestors continued to play a part in their lives. They made figures of ancestors, which they consulted and worshiped by making offerings to them. They also believed that the figures housed the ancestors' souls and so prevented them from wandering and possibly having a bad effect on people's lives.

1. & 2. *Senufo ancestors*, Ivory Coast; 3. *Baule ancestor*, Ivory Coast; 4. *Babuye ancestor*, Zaire (Metropolitan Museum of Art, New York).

♦ MASKS

Masks were used in initiation ceremonies and by members of secret societies. They had no realistic features, but rather suggested something supernatural.

1. *Baule mask*, Ivory Coast;
2. *Kwele mask*, Congo Republic;
3. *Senufo mask*, Ivory Coast (Musée des Arts Africains et Océaniens, Paris).

1

2

3

1

2

3

♦ MOTHERHOOD

Motherhood is a common subject of African sculpture. Fertility was synonymous with prosperity.

1. *Bakongo woman*, Zaire (Museo Pigorini, Rome);
2. *Dan mother*, Nigeria (Musée des Arts Africains et Océaniens);
3. *Yoruba mother*, Nigeria (Metropolitan Museum of Art, New York).

2

3

4

1

5

6

7

♦ THE IFE AND BENIN BRONZES

A refined method of bronze casting was developed in the Ife and Benin kingdoms. Kings and queens and other dignitaries were represented. Ife works seem realistic enough to be true portraits. Benin examples are more decorated, showing ornaments worn around the neck, and the forehead covered by a cap.

(1. Museum für Völkerkunde, Berlin; 2. Museum Reitburg, Zurich; 3. Field Museum of Natural History, Chicago; 4. Metropolitan Museum of Art, New York; 5. Musée des Arts Africains et Océaniens, Paris; 6. Museum für Völkerkunde, Berlin; 7. Metropolitan Museum of Art, New York.)

♦ NOK HEAD
From the Nok culture (National Museum, Lagos).

♦ AFRICAN ART
The most ancient African sculptures date back to the middle of the 1st millennium BC when, in central Nigeria, the Nok civilization prospered. Most of the works were in terracotta – life-size heads with highly stylized features. The eyes, mouth, nostrils and ears were shown with holes. Between the 11th and the 15th centuries, the powerful Ife kingdom became established in south-west Nigeria. Artists from the Ife culture working in terracotta or bronze portrayed humans in a realistic way. The bronze heads of kings and queens were true portraits. Artists in the later kingdom of Benin, which developed in southern Nigeria between the 13th and the 19th centuries, were partly influenced by the Ife. A series of bronze works from both kingdoms were found near Tada. One is outstanding for the skill of the sculptor in achieving the natural appearance of a figure sitting cross-legged.

♦ MODERN ARTISTS TAKE AN INTEREST
In the early 20th century Western artists wanted to break from their own traditions of representing the world as it really looks. They took great interest in the art of other cultures. Stylized African sculpture, which had been considered just a curiosity, became an inspiration for the abstract work of modern artists.
Far left: *Mask* (Musée Barbier-Müller, Geneva); Left: Max Ernst, *The King Playing with the Queen* (Galerie Beyeler, Basel).

♦ SEATED FIGURE
Copper figure, 13th-14th century, found at Tada (National Museum, Lagos).

THE 20TH CENTURY

Each age of human history can be seen as having been dominated by a single style of art. For centuries, in ancient Greece and Rome, artists produced classical art. In later times, the Romanesque, Renaissance, Baroque and Neoclassical styles have been dominant, and each has lasted for many decades, or even for centuries. This slow succession of styles has been replaced, in the 20th century, by a rapid succession of trends.

The work of early 20th-century artists expressed a desire for radical change and freedom from the traditional rules of naturalistic portrayal. Each great artist, influenced by the experience of the world wars, by modern industry and communication, and by contact with other cultures, seems to have developed his or her own way of understanding and producing art. The examples here represent some of the many 20th-century movements including Cubism, Dada, Surrealism, Pop Art, Packaging Art and Land Art.

✦ 1961
CLAES OLDENBURG, *Roast Beef* (Sonnabend Collection, New York).

✦ 1938
HENRY MOORE, *Composition* (Private collection).

✦ 1964
ANDY WARHOL, *Kellogg's Cornflakes Box* (Sonnabend Collection, New York). Pop Art introduced goods from the industrial world into the world of art.

1983 ✦
GEORGE SEGAL, *Rush hour* (Sidney Janis Gallery, New York). Crowded together, but each person shut inside his own solitude.

1943 ✦
PABLO PICASSO, *Bull* (Musée Picasso, Paris). A bull's head made from two bicycle parts.

✦ 1903
HENRI MATISSE, *Madeleine II* (Musée Matisse, Nice). Without arms, the figure has hardly been formed. The shape seems to be slowly dissolving.

1909 ✦
PABLO PICASSO, *Head of a Woman* (Kunsthaus, Zurich). The Cubist shape breaks down into several intersecting blocks.

1913 ✦
MARCEL DUCHAMP, *Bicycle Wheel*, replica of the original. The artist chose an ordinary object and displayed it as art. He called this type of work a "ready-made".

1960 ✦
ALBERTO GIACOMETTI, *Man walking* (Maeght Foundation, Saint-Paul-de-Vence).

1960 ✦
CHRISTO, A packaged public building. The idea of "Packaging Art" was that hiding something made it more conspicuous.

♦ 1910
CONSTANTIN BRANCUSI, *The Kiss* (Musée National d'Art Moderne, Paris). Interest in primitive culture prompted a return to essential, stylized shapes.

1911 ♦
AMEDEO MODIGLIANI, *Head* (Tate Gallery, London). He took to sculpture after meeting Brancusi. The heads he sculpted were inspired by African masks.

1912 ♦
UMBERTO BOCCIONI, *Development of a Bottle in Space* (Private collection, Milan). The Futurists tried to express the energy of the machine age in their art. Here, the bottle, the plate and the table are one piece moving through space.

♦ 1919
RAOUL HAUSMAN, *The Spirit of our Time* (Georges Pompidou Centre, Paris). A series of mechanical objects are assembled on a wig stand. The Dada movement ridiculed modern professions.

1932 ♦
HANS ARP, *Giant Seed* (Musée National d'Art Moderne, Paris). An abstract shape which suggested something from nature.

1936 ♦
MERET OPPENHEIM *Lunch in Fur* (Museum of Modern Art, New York). Surrealist sculpture.

1936 ♦
SALVADOR DALI, *Venus with Drawers* (Private collection, Paris). A classical work is reinvented as an improbable object for everyday use. Surrealism totally rejected the rules of logic and blended fantasy and reality.

♦ 1950
ETTORE COLLA in his motorized cart, collecting scrap metal from which he made sculptures of machines. Creating art from industrial scrap was typical of post-war sculpture.

♦ 1963
CLAES OLDENBURG, *Prawns on forks*, plaster, wood and plastic foam (Musée d'Art Contemporain, Nice).

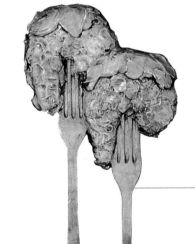

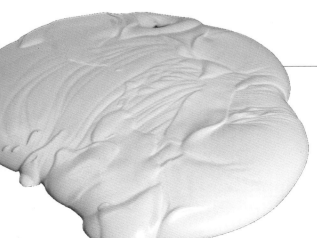

♦ 1970
CÉSAR, *Untitled*. The introduction of plastic revolutionized the world of sculpture.

1970 ♦
ROBERT SMITHSON, *Spiral Jetty*, Great Salt Lake, Utah. Land Art or Earthworks meant sculpting the actual environment.

SCULPTURE AND TECHNOLOGY

In every period of history, the tools and materials available and the skills and understanding of the time have influenced the kind of work that sculptors have produced. The fast development of technology in the 20th century has opened up many possibilities. New materials, such as plastics, and new tools, including computers and lasers, have allowed artists to be extremely innovative. Enormous sculptures assembled from iron and steel are monuments to modern technology. The discovery of how an object can stand upright, resting on a single point, or hang in mid-air from one thread, suggested different ways in which a sculpture could occupy space. The American sculptor Alexander Calder was the first to make sculptures which actually moved. Many modern sculptors design their works, creating models in their studios. Often, the sculpture itself is produced from this model by craftspeople in workshops or large, industrial assembly shops.

♦THUMB
This sculpture on the coast road in Jeddah, Saudi Arabia, was enlarged from a model of the *Thumb of King Fahd*, by the French sculptor César. In a workshop in Carrara, Italy, the model was enlarged to the size of a block of marble weighing 36 tons. Using the method of measuring distances between reference points on the original model, and multiplying them, it is possible to create an exact but greatly magnified copy.

MARBLE ♦
The marble is shaped by technical experts who are able to produce a work of art without the artist being involved in any of the practical work.

REFERENCE POINTS ♦
Reference points are fixed on the model. Distances between them are measured and multiplied up, according to how many times bigger than the model the final work is to be.

PLASTER MODEL ♦
The plaster model is a copy of the artist's design. The technicians follow its measurements and all details minutely, in order to achieve a perfect enlargement.

ALEXANDER CALDER ✦
Calder (1898-1976) trained as a mechanical engineer. His first moving sculptures, named "mobiles", were worked by hand or motor, but later ones responded to air movement. They were made from his models in industrial workshops.

✦ MOVEMENT
In the past, statues may have conveyed a feeling of movement, but the objects themselves were solidly immobile. The introduction of moving parts was a significant stage in the development of sculpture. Electronic programming made it possible for spectators to activate an object's moving parts. In 1966, Robert Breer created a series of sculptures that reacted as soon as they were approached.

GREAT SPEED ✦
Alexander Calder, 1969. Painted steel, height 13 meters (43 feet). Vanderberg Center Plaza, Grand Rapids, Michigan, USA.

♦ INDEX